"What does God promise us, and what does it look like to believe him? In her thorough examination of Sarah's life and faith, Shannon shows us what it means to be shaped by God's promises—to live like everything God says is true. Here you will find an in-depth searching of Scripture, valuable insights, and help for growing in your faith, ultimately because Shannon will point you to Jesus, the perfect promise-shaped Son."

    —**Kristen Wetherell**, author of *Help for the Hungry Soul* and
    Fight Your Fears

"For the woman waiting on God, wondering when he'll answer or wrestling over why he's taking so long, Shannon offers fresh hope in Scripture, reminding you that you are never forgotten, forsaken, or overlooked. Grab a copy of *Shaped by God's Promises*, allowing God to hold your heart while he holds your hand to guide you into the glorious future he has for you."

    —**Erica Wiggenhorn**, national speaker with Aspire Women's Events
    and award-winning author of *An Unexpected Revival: Experiencing*
    God's Goodness through Disappointment and Doubt

A SIX-WEEK BIBLE STUDY

Shaped by God's Promises

LESSONS FROM SARAH ON FEAR AND FAITH

Shannon Popkin

Our Daily Bread
Publishing.

Shaped by God's Promises: Lessons from Sarah on Fear and Faith
© 2024 by Shannon Popkin

Author is represented by the literary agency of Credo Communications LLC, Grand Rapids, Michigan, www.credocommunications.net.

Requests for permission to quote from this book should be directed to: Permissions Department, Our Daily Bread Publishing, PO Box 3566, Grand Rapids, MI 49501; or contact us by email at permissionsdept@odb.org.

Scripture quotations, unless otherwise indicated, are taken from the ESV® Bible (The Holy Bible, English Standard Version®), copyright © 2001 by Crossway, a publishing ministry of Good News Publishers. Used by permission. All rights reserved.

Scripture quotations marked CSB have been taken from the Christian Standard Bible®, Copyright © 2017 by Holman Bible Publishers. Used by permission. Christian Standard Bible® and CSB® are federally registered trademarks of Holman Bible Publishers.

Scripture quotations marked NIV are taken from the Holy Bible, New International Version®, NIV®. Copyright © 1973, 1978, 1984, 2011 by Biblica, Inc.™ Used by permission of Zondervan. All rights reserved worldwide. www.zondervan.com.

Interior design by Jody Langley

ISBN: 978-1-64070-307-0

Library of Congress Cataloging-in-Publication Data Available

Printed in the United States of America
24 25 26 27 28 29 30 31 / 8 7 6 5 4 3 2 1

Contents

To my parents, Roger and Judie Berry

Your love for God's promises created a foundation for my faith.

How to Be Shaped by God's Promises

God's promises aren't like mine; just ask my kids. I used to tell them, "I promise I'll pick you up on time today. I *promise.*" But then there would be a traffic backup. Or I'd drop a carton of eggs just before getting out the door. Or I'd bump into a friend at the grocery store and lose track of time as we chatted away. My promises were often derailed by unforeseen circumstances that prevented me from keeping them.

God, however, doesn't have unforeseen circumstances. He has control over the whole world and everything in it, which means he *can* keep every one of his promises. And he does!

God's promises are like a set of parentheses. When he makes a promise, he lays down the first parenthesis, and when he keeps the promise, he closes the set. Like parentheses, God's promises always come in pairs; you never have one without the other. But often, there is far more space between the parentheses than we expect.

Now, because these promises come from God (not your chronically late mom), you can cling to them tightly, with great expectation—and I hope you do! But clinging to the promises isn't the hard part.

A Thinner Story

As God's people, we're often big fans of the promises. We love to rehearse them and comfort ourselves with what is to come. We have t-shirts and tumblers inscribed with the phrase, "God always keeps his promises." What we don't like, however, is the gap on the timeline between the two parentheses. We don't want to experience the "cling in between." We'd rather just pull the parentheses in close.

promise made   promise kept

(time)

I've created some lists of promises for you in the back of the book, which I'll be referring to throughout the study. Appendix 1 on page 287 offers you three questions to ask yourself when approaching the promises. (Hint: Not all of the promises are for all people.) Appendix 2 on page 291 divides up the promises into three lists, with room for you to add more as you discover them in your Bible. Take a minute to familiarize yourself with this section of the book.

The reality? There are many promises from God that we won't see fulfilled in our lifetime. Try putting that on a tumbler. It's uncomfortable. We don't like it. We have Amazon expectations of next-day delivery.

To soothe our agitation, we mentally collapse the timeline and pull the parentheses in close—even in the way we read the Bible. Just think about the songs we sing, the memes we create, and the conversations we have. We delete that huge gap between Genesis 3 and Matthew 1 and jump from sin to the cross, all in the same sentence.

Now, I understand the sentiment. Who wants to linger on sin and death (introduced by Adam and Eve) when you can flip over to forgiveness and eternal life (provided by Jesus)? Yet here's my question: Is it okay to reduce our Bibles to a much thinner story? I doubt any of us would physically rip out the parts in the middle to create a simpler, cleaner storyline. But when we force the parentheses in tight, wanting to skip to the good part, do we lose anything?

Have you spent more time studying the Old Testament or New Testament of your Bible? Why?

....

....

....

....

What might be lost if we skipped the parts of our Bible leading up to Jesus's birth?

....

....

....

....

....

What might be gained if we lingered?*

....

....

....

....

....

*In this third question, I'm asking you to "infer," or to reason and draw out implications based on what you already know about the Bible. If you are just beginning to study the Bible or don't have any thoughts about that particular question (or others like it in this study), I don't want you to get bogged down. Perhaps something you read later will trigger an idea, and you can return to it. If you need permission to leave some questions blank, it's yours. There's value in considering and pondering, even if you don't have a tidy answer, and that's what questions like this one are meant to prompt.

Don't Skip the Good Part

In this six-week study of the life of Sarah, we'll study Genesis 12–21, which falls in that long stretch of time between the initial sin and the life of Jesus.

Back in Genesis 3:15, in the wake of evil entering the world, God promised that the woman's offspring would crush the snake and eradicate evil. Then, after hundreds of years pass, God opens another set of parentheses* and promises to bless all the nations of the world through a man named Abram (Genesis 12:3). It's still early in the overarching story of the Bible, so Abram and his wife Sarai have lots of unanswered questions on how and when God will keep this promise. However, it seems they know that somewhere along the line, their family tree (which currently has no branches) will produce the promised snake-crushing Savior (John 8:56).

Let's stop and think for a moment. Why is the story of "the Abrams" (as I like to call them) even necessary to the plot? Couldn't we scoop out the centuries it takes God to "make of [Abram] a great nation" (Genesis 12:2), and skip to the good part where Jesus comes to die for our sin?

I hope that by the end of this study, you'll be convinced that the stretch between the parentheses *is* one of the good parts. But for now, let me assure you: God, the author of the Bible, has good things in mind when he inserts long stretches of time between making and keeping his promises.

Yes, this is grammatically impossible, but work with me!

promise made   promise kept

time

(The Tension of an Open Parenthesis

If you're a grammar girl, you probably find this unpaired parenthesis in my heading annoying. (Here, I'll close one for you.) But consider how it also holds your attention. Does it feel like a cupboard door is open and needs to be closed? That's how we're meant to feel when we read God's promises in the Bible that have not been fulfilled. Each unpaired parenthesis is meant to hold our attention and build our anticipation for what's to come.

My husband and I had the opposite experience last week when we decided to try a Netflix show our daughter had recommended. We started watching it without realizing she had signed into her account on our TV, so without meaning to, we picked up where she had left off—which was the fifth season. By the time we discovered our mistake, we had stumbled upon several key plot details. When we started over in Season One, these spoilers made the show far less exciting.

God is a masterful storyteller who doesn't spoil things by skipping too quickly to future "seasons." As the story unfolds slowly, with yet-unfulfilled promises, tension builds and our attention is held. These open parentheses feel like a song with no final note or a book with no final page. As we turn the pages of our Bible, we wonder, *Can God keep his promises? Will he?*

This is the main tension in the story of Sarah. We're first introduced to her this way: "Now Sarai was barren; she had no child" (Genesis 11:30). Then, only verses later, God promises her husband, "I will make of you a great nation" (Genesis 12:2).

Can you imagine Sarai's heart leaping with glee? If Abram was to be the father of a nation, this meant Sarai would be the *mother* of a nation! The first parenthesis had been put in place. But then came her next period (not the punctuation sort). And the next, and the next, until there were no more. And we wonder along with Sarai, *Can God keep his promises? Will he?* Supposing we believe he will, a new question emerges as the gap between the parentheses widens: *Why is God waiting so long?*

What are you waiting for God to do in your life or in the life of someone you love?

....

....

....

....

How has this waiting time been one of the "good parts"? How has God used this to get or hold your attention?

....

....

....

....

....

The Why behind the Wait

I've divided Sarah's story (Sarai at first), into six study weeks. In our first four lessons of each week, we'll dig into the narrative and consider both Sarah's and God's perspectives on what unfolds. Then in the fifth lesson of each week, I'll give you an opportunity to retell Sarah's story (it's so good to make these stories retrievable for later) and reflect on how God is inviting you, too, to be shaped by his promises.

One of the greatest tensions we'll encounter in Sarah's story is time. Time is slipping by, making it increasingly unlikely that God's promises will ever be fulfilled. And the unspoken question that grows like a crescendo is, *Why, God? Why the wait?*

I'll invite you to wrestle with this tension in your own story as you observe it in Sarah's.

Have you ever struggled with that long stretch between the parentheses? Have you longed for injustices to be made right? Have you agonized over the lack of evidence that he is working anything together for good (Romans 8:28)? I certainly have. A while back, I bought a five-year prayer journal that provides a page for each day of the year to record your prayers. In Year Two, you can look back at your prayer from the previous year on that day. Once, after recording a particularly agonizing request to God in the journal, I looked back on my prayer from that same day a few years before and realized my plea was almost identical. Word for word, I was crying out to God for exactly what I had already requested. Do you have any "on repeat" prayer requests you've been bringing to God, literally for years?

God often uses the open parentheses to hold our attention and turn our focus to him. My prayer journal is tangible evidence of the "cling in between" the parentheses of God's promises. God frequently lifts my eyes to him while I wait on him. Have you experienced this, too?

Certain purposes of God can *only* be accomplished between a set of widely placed parentheses. As you study, keep the following two purposes in mind, both of which are demonstrated in Sarah's story. Keep them in mind for yourself, too, as you navigate the wide space between the promises made and the promises kept by God.

1. God's Faithfulness Is Proven over Time

Suppose I showed you a photo and said, "Here's a man I met today who is so faithful." You might think that was an odd thing to say. How could I possibly know if someone I just met is faithful? But what if I showed you the same photo and said, "Here's my husband of twenty-six years. He's so faithful." Now I have more credibility, right?

You see, faithfulness is only demonstrated over time.

As we study Sarah's life and the promises God made and kept to her, we're going to learn about God's faithfulness in a way we couldn't if our Bibles skipped straight from Genesis 3 to Matthew 1. In some instances, decades will elapse between the promises God makes and keeps. In other instances, we're still waiting (along with Sarah) for God to close the parentheses.

In every paragraph of Sarah's life, God is showing us that he is faithful. And in the pages that follow, we see that God is willing to spend thousands of years on the Bible's timeline to demonstrate what a thinner Bible couldn't: His faithfulness.

But God doesn't just want us to know *about* his faithfulness. He wants us to know him personally, as a faithful, covenant-keeping God. Think of my photo analogy. If my new "faithful" acquaintance promised to deposit $1,000 into my checking account, I'd be a fool to give him my account number, right? But if my husband promised this, I'd probably start planning how to spend it.

Our faithful God delights in our plans to "spend" what he has promised. He wants his promises to make a personal difference in our lives, which brings us to our second anchoring truth.

2. God Wants Us to Be Shaped by His Promises

One of the things I'm excited for you to discover in Sarah's story is how her character shifts over time. You'll see her go from being a fretting, controlling, insecure, self-focused woman to a confident, secure woman of God who takes a great risk and is filled with laughter and joy. What makes the difference? This verse encapsulates it nicely:

> [Sarah] considered him faithful who had promised.
> (Hebrews 11:11)

Do you see that word *consider*? It's an accounting term. Think of a banker *considering* your loan application and weighing the evidence to decide. So when Sarah examines God from various angles on the timeline, she considers him to be faithful, and this is what changes her. As Sarah watches God keep his promises, she comes to expect the pattern to continue.

Sarah is shaped by the promises of God, which is what God wants for you as well. Sarah's story wasn't only meant for Sarah; it's one of the good parts of the story, meant for you and me. As you read and study, feel the hug of God's faithfulness as the parentheses close in Sarah's life, and watch for his faithfulness in your own life. God wants you to become a woman who—even in the waiting—can be described as Sarah was:

_____ **considered him faithful who had promised.**

Put your name in that blank and read it out loud. Do you want this to be true of you? Then open your Bible to one of the good parts in Genesis 12 and get ready to be shaped by God's promises.

Timelines and Maps

Overarching Story

God calls
Abram
Genesis 12

430 years
Galatians 3:17

The Exodus
Exodus 12

Moses writes
Genesis

1500 years

Jesus died
and rose

Church is born
at Pentecost

Sarah's Timeline

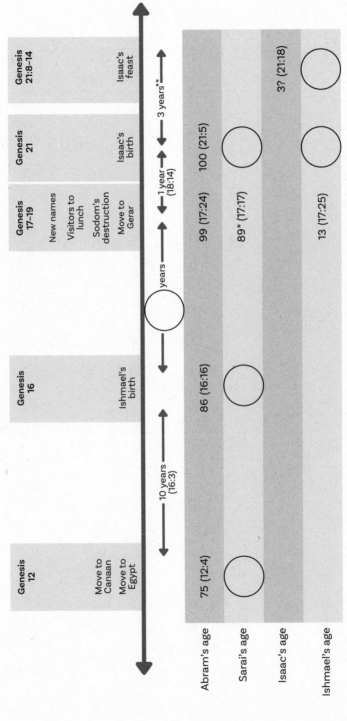

	Genesis 12	Genesis 16		Genesis 17-19	Genesis 21	Genesis 21:8-14
	Move to Canaan Move to Egypt	Ishmael's birth		New names Visitors to lunch Sodom's destruction Move to Gerar	Isaac's birth	Isaac's feast

10 years (16:3) — years — 1 year (18:14) — 3 years**

Abram's age	75 (12:4)	86 (16:16)	99 (17:24)	100 (21:5)
Sarai's age			89* (17:17)	
Isaac's age				3? (21:18)
Ishmael's age			13 (17:25)	

*Abram does the math in Genesis 17:17; nine month from now, they would be 90 and 100

**Children were often weaned between ages 3 and 4

Map of Ancient Mesopotamia and the Middle East

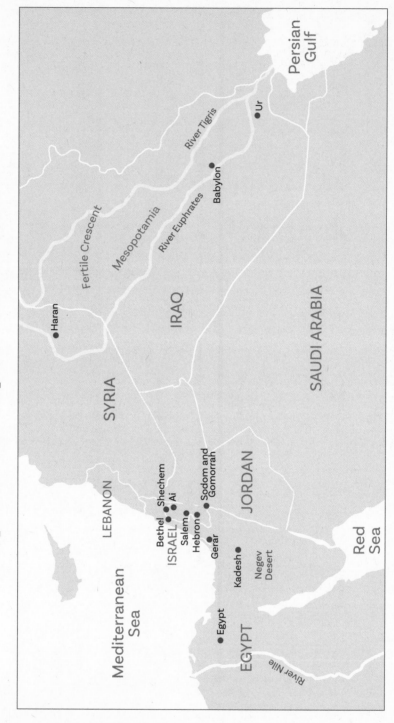

● = Ancient cities   ALL CAPS = Modern countries

The People of the Promise

The People of the Promise

The God Who Says, "I Will"

Back in my twenties, I agreed for my friend to set me up on a blind date with a guy from our church. In the weeks prior, I asked several trusted friends, "What do you know about this guy, Ken?" Nobody knew much. He worked out of town. He didn't come to the social gatherings. One friend, Chris, was one of the pastors and had met Ken, so he said he'd point him out.

The next Sunday, across the crowded church atrium, I saw Chris waving to me and pointing at Ken. Chris always laughs when I describe how I ducked out of sight, mortified. That glimpse was enough, though, to help me identify Ken later that day, as we were about to pass—just the two of us—on the church stairwell. *Would he say hello? Should I mention the date?* But the handsome, mysterious stranger passed me by without even making eye contact.

Well, the date went well. Ken made me laugh. I liked him. So I proceeded with caution and, over time, he proved to be a considerate, generous, attentive man who loved God and loved me. Within a year, my blind date had become my best friend, so when he popped the question, I said yes.

The Origin Story of God's People

In the opening of Abram and Sarai's story, God is like a mysterious stranger. No one they trusted knew anything about him because slowly, across the face of the earth, the knowledge of God had been snuffed out. *How can that be?* we wonder. *Didn't God just create the world a few pages back?*

Yes, and that's sort of the point.

You see, Genesis is an origin story. Part One of the book (Genesis 1–11) opens with God walking and talking with Adam and Eve in a beautiful garden. Then the serpent recruits them for a rebellion, they commit treason, and tragic consequences ensue. Adam and Eve are separated from God, and sin-soaked corruption and death spread like a blight, passed on to each new generation.

Part One closes with Adam and Eve's descendants flexing for the world by building a tower in a town called Babel. God shuts the operation down by confusing their language and dispersing them into new family clans that scatter across the face of the earth and eventually become the nations. (You can read the story in Genesis 11:1–9).

Then comes Part Two, the origin story of God's people, which opens with God selecting one of those dispersed family clans to commit himself to: a childless couple named Abram and Sarai.

A Chosen Family

Read Genesis 11:27–29 and fill out Abram's family tree, beginning with his father, Terah.

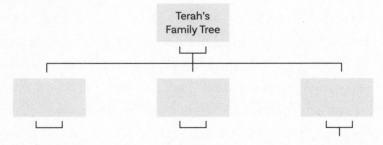

What hints are given about why God chose Abram? Consider Joshua 24:2 as you answer.

....

....

....

Read Genesis 12:1–4 and briefly summarize the promises God makes about:

Blessing ....

....

....

Offspring ....

....

....

Nation ....

....

....

What additional promise does God make in Genesis 12:7?

....

....

....

These were some astonishing promises! To be "blessed" implies Abram will be wealthy and have a bright future filled with things going his way.[1] To have a great name implies that people far and wide will not only know of Abram, but think highly of him. Not to mention a nation-sized family and a destiny to bless the whole world. Um . . . yes, please!

Sarai isn't mentioned specifically here, but she's likely pretty pleased about these jaw-dropping promises that will change her life in a big way.

A Proposal

The origin story for God's people begins here, with two people whose lives are about to change drastically. Since the Bible often uses marriage as a metaphor to describe God's relationship with us, we might call this the "blind date" of the relationship—but it reads more like a proposal. The pace is dizzying. There is no asking around or proceeding with caution. Abram is simply told, "Go from your land, your relatives, and your father's house" (Genesis 12:1 CSB). Can you imagine? It's as jarring as it would have been that day on the church stairwell if the handsome stranger had looked up at me and said, "Let's get married. Go get packed and I'll show you where to go."

Set aside any "proposal imagery" from your culture (such as a boy on his knee or a photographer around the corner capturing the girl's surprise) and think about what marriage proposals have in common.

In a proposal, what is proposed, stated, and implied?

....

....

....

How does responding "yes" require faith?

....

....

....

How does Genesis 12:1–4 remind you of a proposal?

....

....

What is surprising about this proposal?

....

....

....

....

....

....

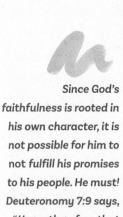

I Will, I Will, I Will

Most proposals begin with, "Will you . . . ?" But God begins with a series of, "I will . . ." promise statements. These promises are not only amazing because of what is promised, but because of who is doing the promising. Think about the back-story.

Nothing is said about the Abrams seeking after God. As you read in Joshua 24:2, their family served other gods. They were likely moon-worshipers.[2] So Abram was just living his moon-worshiping life when God showed up, promising to bless him.

What, then, is the origin story for God's people? It began with God saying, "I will."

In Genesis 12:1–4, how many times does God say, "I will"?

....

....

Who will keep the promises, and who will benefit from them? What does this say about God's relationship with us?

....

....

....

....

God Walks the Aisle

If Genesis 12 is the proposal story, then Genesis 15 is the marriage ceremony. It comes a little further into the story, but let's take a look.

God tells Abram that—like the stars in the sky—his offspring will be too numerous to count. They will possess the land under his feet. "How will I know?" Abram asks (see Genesis 15:8). In response, God tells Abram to cut some animals in two and lay the pieces in rows, facing each other, with an "aisle" in between.

Now, if you or I saw a neighbor laying animal pieces on their front lawn, we'd probably call Animal Protection. But back then, this was how people "cut" covenant. The two parties would walk the aisle between the severed animal pieces, as if to say, "May it be to me like these animals if I break my promises to you." This, by the way, is where we get the idea of "walking the aisle" in a marriage ceremony[3] (only without the gore).

Read Genesis 15:12, 17–18. How does this covenant ceremony deviate from what I described above? (Hint: Note what Abram is doing in verse 12.)

....

....

....

....

What was God demonstrating to Abram? What does this imply about our relationship with God?

....

....

....

....

It Starts with Promises

Imagine attending a wedding where only the groom walked the aisle and made the covenant promises to a bride who hasn't even cleaned herself up. We would be wondering things, right? We should have a similar sense of wonder as we consider this covenant between God and his people.

God's relationship with Abram creates a pattern or "type" for the rest of us who have been born into sinful corruption and can't clean ourselves up enough to pursue God. So how can we ever go from being God's enemies to God's people? Like with Abram, it begins with a set of lavish, astonishing, loving, glorious promises made—not by us, but God.

Now, God does ask Abram to obey. And God will make other promises to his people which are conditional on them obeying his laws. But the Bible emphasizes that those laws didn't come until 430 years *after* God made these promises to Abram (see Galatians 3:17). The point is: our relationship with God begins with him making promises and committing to keep them—and us responding in faith.

Does this ring true for you? It does for me. I remember the day, at age four, when I was playing in our front yard under the birch tree. I was thinking about the story of Nicodemus—the guy who didn't want to die. I didn't want to die either, so I thought carefully about what Jesus promised this man: "Whoever believes in me will have eternal life" (see

John 3:16). I went inside and told my mom that I wanted to believe in Jesus, too! I wanted to live.

That life-changing decision began with me considering God's promises.

When you first turned to God (or as you've considered doing so), what promises were you responding to? Perhaps a promise about being forgiven, accepted by God, or receiving eternal life? Or maybe you were wisely disturbed by God's promise to judge sin.

Tell about the earliest promise from God you remember responding to, and why. (You can refer to the list on page 291.)

....

....

....

....

I hope that through this study, God's promises will become increasingly precious to you. But here's what you might not realize: If you belong to God, then *you* are one of the ways God has kept his promises to Abram and Sarai. Your story is linked to theirs.

Children of Nations

Look up Genesis 12:3 in the CSB* version:

All the _____ on _____ will be

_____ through you.

*From time to time, I'll ask you to look up a Bible verse in a translation that might be less familiar to you. You can go to sites like www.biblegateway .com for free access to these translations.

Who are the "peoples" or families God is referring to?

....

....

What did God also promise Abraham in Genesis 17:5?

....

....

....

If the Bible were a story about God making promises exclusively to Abram and his descendants, it would be pretty devastating for the rest of the nations that had dispersed at Babel, wouldn't it? For centuries, that's actually how it looked. Then one special day, God blew open the doors and made a way for people of all nations to become "children of Abraham."

On Pentecost (a Jewish holiday that fell fifty days after Jesus's resurrection), Jesus's disciples—filled with God's Spirit—began speaking in languages they did not know. It was like the Tower of Babel, only with the reverse effect. People gathered, hearing their own languages, and a huge crowd formed to hear a sermon about God's Son, Jesus, who died on the cross—not for his sin, but theirs. Jesus's death could count as their penalty. His blood could wash away their sin's corruption. By God's grace, Jesus's eternal life and inheritance could be theirs to share! They simply had to believe God's promises about this way to be saved.

What is said about the nations (or families) in:

    Acts 2:5–6 ....

....

    Genesis 12:3 ....

....

Genesis 17:5 ....
....

How is God keeping his promises in Acts 2:41?

....

....

....

Back when God promised that all the nations would be blessed through Abram, I think it was like a ten-second preview of *this* day, when Abram became the father of many nations (Romans 4:17). God wanted those of us who are Irish, Mexican, Chinese, and Swahili to know we weren't an afterthought. Back when God was saying, "I will . . ." to Abram, he wasn't excluding you. He was *including* you in his plans. Through Abram came Jesus—who was sent to bless *you* (Genesis 12:3).

After Pentecost, as believers of every nation returned home carrying God's promises with them, the message about Jesus began to spread throughout the world. It has spread even to me and you. Here's a quote from that Pentecost sermon:

> The promise is for you and for your children, and for all who are far off, as many as the Lord our God will call. (Acts 2:39 CSB).

Did you see that? This promise is for you! Add your name in that blank:

"The promise is for_____."

Faith Is Going without Knowing

When Heather's parents became missionaries in Mongolia, people wondered, "Is that even responsible? You have eight kids! What if you need medical help?" Faith required going without knowing all the answers.

Listen to more of Heather Cofer's story on Shannon's Live Like It's True podcast. Go to shannonpopkin.com /promises.

On Heather's twelfth birthday, her mom was experiencing pregnancy complications and needed to be airlifted to China. Amidst the chaos of medical people arriving and her mom being moved on a stretcher, Heather's dad pulled her aside. "Heather, I know this is scary and hard for you. But you have an opportunity to show your younger siblings what it looks like to bring your fear to the Lord and trust him." So that's what she chose to do.

Twelve-year-old Heather used her limited grasp of the Mongolian language and culture to help her grandparents (who happened to be visiting) navigate the city, take a taxi to the embassy for visas, and care for siblings who had chicken pox. Heather still recalls how her faith grew as God brought her baby sister safely into the world.

Now, I hear this and want to shield Heather's young faith—maybe by distracting her with cake or presents. It's fascinating to me that her dad did the opposite. Instead of coddling Heather, he commissioned his believing daughter to have "going without knowing" faith, which is what God asks of all of us. Even missionaries to Mongolia. Even twelve-year-olds. Even you.

In the previous lesson, we noted that God was the one making and keeping the promises. Yet he wanted Abram and Sarai to respond to those promises in a big way.

Read Genesis 12:1–4.

How would our origin story be different if verses 2–3 were missing?

....

....

....

....

How would our origin story be different if verses 1 and 4 were missing?

....

....

....

What do we learn about the relationship between faith and obedience?

....

....

....

Use your timeline on page 17 and determine how old Abram and Sarai were.

....

This was no small journey. Abram and Sarai walked a thousand miles to get to the promised land. From where I live in Michigan, it is about a thousand miles to McKinney, Texas (a suburb of Dallas). Find a location a thousand miles from where you live and record it here:

Read Genesis 12:4–8. On your map on page 18, mark the movements that Abram and his clan made.

What do Abram and Sarai's age and the distance they traveled emphasize about their obedience and faith?

....

....

....

....

Putting Feet to Your Faith

Faith begins not with doing some astonishing thing, but with believing some astonishing promise, then living like it's true. Without God's promises, the Abrams would have been crazy to walk a thousand miles into the unknown. But *with* God's promises, they would have been crazy not to.

You and I usually think of "faith" as what we believe about God—so faith is something we do with our heads. But in Hebrew (the language of Genesis), faith is something you do—not just with your head, but also with your feet. The Hebrew word for faith (*emunah*) always carries the idea of both belief and action, together.[4] So if you have faith in the car, you'll drive it. If you have faith in the bridge, you'll walk on it. We are shaped by God's promises when we put feet to our faith.

We see this idea in Hebrews 11, which lists not what great people of faith believed about God, but what they did as a result. The author includes Abram and Sarai's story in its entirety.

1. What did Abram (later called Abraham) do by faith, according to Hebrews 11:8?

....

....

....

What faith-requiring detail is included?

....

....

....

2. What else did Abram do by faith, according to Hebrews 11:9?

....

....

....

How did Abram exhibit faith by not doing something, according to Hebrews 11:15?

....

....

....

What faith-requiring detail is included in Genesis 12:6?

....

....

....

3. Which of these two faith-requiring details do you think was more challenging and why?

....

....

....

....

....

....

Unexpected ~~Blessing~~ Testing

After Abram and Sarai make this thousand-mile "going without knowing" journey, then arrive in a foreign country, I'm looking around for those big blessings God promised. I kind of expect a "Blessing Bus" to pull up in front of their tent, loaded up with high chairs and strollers for all those kids they'll be having. But instead of getting blessed, they get a test.

Genesis 12:5–6 says, "When they came to the land of Canaan, Abram passed through the land . . ." Then it tells where they landed on the map and adds one small detail:

> **At that time _____ were in the land.**
> **(Genesis 12:6)**

They've come a thousand miles, banking on what God had promised. If it were me, I'd be picturing a big, empty, undiscovered land to claim, wouldn't you? I suppose they felt a little foolish when they found Canaanites acting like they owned the place. I can just see the withering worry and alarm spreading across Sarai's face as the second parenthesis gets moved out on the timeline—extended by a long stretch of "not yet."

promise made

(◄─────────────────────────────► not yet . . .

So we're learning that part of God's way for us to be shaped by his promises involves tests. Sometimes the test involves putting feet to our faith. Other times, the test involves staying put—even when there are reasons not to.

How has God been testing you instead of blessing you? Tell about a time (present or past) when you faced each of these situations:

God gave you something, then took it away

....

....

....

God took longer than you thought

....

....

....

There was some unexpected threat

....

....

....

God led you somewhere, but it didn't turn out like you expected

....

....

....

Which of these situations tempted you to turn back, instead of staying put?

....

....

....

....

....

In seasons of "not yet," there is such temptation to turn back, but Abram and Sarai not only obeyed, they stayed. They not only left home, they didn't return home when the second parenthesis didn't close on God's promises immediately.

Meet the Wildernites

Stop with me for a moment and consider the first audience of Genesis—the descendants of Abram and Sarai who now number about two million people. I call them the "Wildernites" because they are the Israelites living in the wilderness. (As you can tell, I like nicknames. But I also want to help you place the original audience of Genesis on the timeline.) When Moses wrote Genesis, he was thinking of them, not us. In fact, Moses might be surprised to think of women across the world, thousands of years later, reading his stuff. Considering what Sarai's story meant to the Wildernites will help us keep from adding or detracting from its meaning for us.

Look at the timeline on page 16.

ISRAEL/HEBREWS/ JEWS … HUH? The (eventual) descendants of Abram and Sarai are called Israelites, after Israel (the name God gives to Jacob, grandson of Abram). They are also referred to as the Hebrews, after their language and descent. In addition, they're called Jews, perhaps after the tribe of Judah.

Genesis was written about how many years after Abram was given the promise?

....

Had any of the Wildernites met Abram and Sarai?

....

....

To seat ourselves among the Wildernites, we have to understand their backstory. They were slaves in Egypt for hundreds of years before God set them free. It's an amazing story of God splitting the Red Sea and leading them all the way to the cusp of the promised land, which he had first promised to Abram. If Genesis 12 was the proposal story, this is God carrying his people over the threshold into their new life together.

However, when the people arrived in Canaan, they got the same test instead of blessing that Abram and Sarai had: there were still Canaanites living in the land, acting like they owned the place. And these Canaanites were so big, they made the people feel like grasshoppers (Numbers 13:33).

Go to your big timeline and add a star for the times the Abrams and the Israelites first entered Canaan.

Read Numbers 14:1–4.

What two things do the people moan about in Numbers 14:2?

If only ... .

....

If only ... .

....

In verse 3, they ask, "Why is the Lord bringing us _____ _____

_____?"

What is the answer to this question?

....

....

....

....

What do they say to each other in verse 4, and why?

....

....

....

....

....

A Threshold Disaster

Ken kept our honeymoon plans a surprise. After I changed out of my wedding dress and came out with my suitcase in hand, he embraced me from behind and whispered, "Are you ready to go to Cape Cod?" My heart danced with excitement. My handsome new groom had been nothing but honorable and trustworthy. Why wouldn't I ride off into the sunset with him?

Now imagine if things went differently. Suppose I got my first glimpse of Cape Cod and started crying and trembling, saying, "I'm not going. There's no way this will end well. I'd rather be dead than go there with *you*. I'm finding some other guy to take me back home."

Well, that would be a threshold disaster, yes? This is what is happening with the Wildernites. They are filled with fear, not faith—so much so, they'd rather be dead than cross over into the promised land. Their plan is to ditch God, pick a new leader, and turn back (Numbers 14:2–4).

Back when Abram and Sarai entered this same land, God was like a "new acquaintance" photo (which reveals how extravagant their faith was). But the Wildernites could fill a scrapbook with their experiences of God's faithfulness. Even so, after one glimpse at the promised land, they're trembling in fear, ready to ghost* God and turn back.

*I learned this word from my teens. When you "ghost" someone, you cut off communication without any explanation.

Well, God does not shrug off this threshold disaster (see Numbers 14:26–35). They wish they could die in the wilderness? God's going to make that happen. For forty years they will wander in the wilderness, and only after each adult (age twenty and up) dies, will God lead their children into the promised land. Look at the contrast.

When Abram and Sarai enter the promised land, they've known about God:
   a. A few hundred years
   b. A few months
   c. A few hours

When the Wildernites enter the promised land, they've known about God:
   a. A few hundred years
   b. A few months
   c. A few hours

How have they experienced God's faithfulness over time? Use your prior Bible knowledge and draw lines to all that apply:

Ten plagues

The Red Sea parting

Abram and Sarai

A pillar of cloud and fire to guide them

The Wildernites

Manna from heaven

Water from a rock

What do they encounter upon arriving in the promised land? Draw a line:

Abram and Sarai

Canaanites thinking they own the place

The Wildernites

A "Blessing Bus"

An empty land to occupy

How do Abram and Sarai respond?
   a. They stayed.
   b. They made plans to go back home.

Describe their faith. What can we learn?

....

....

....

....

....

How did the Wildernites respond?
    a. They stayed.
    b. They made plans to go back home.

Describe their faith. What can we learn?

....

....

....

....

....

Ghosting God

Now, let's be fair. It would require incredible bravery for anybody (let alone escaped slaves) to march into some city and say, "It's mine now. God said so." Who wouldn't be terrified? But then, these are the descendants of Abram and Sarai—the ones who famously acted on their faith with their feet. If the Wildernites turned back, would they even *be* the people of the promise anymore?

Amazingly, the answer is yes. God's forty-year consequence isn't given because the people broke their promises. They weren't the ones to *make* the promises in the first place, remember? God's righteous anger burned—not because they ghosted God, but because they doubted him. They refused to be shaped by God's promises.

Look at the exact word God used:

> And your children . . . shall suffer for your _____
> until the last of your dead bodies lies in the wilderness.
> (Numbers 14:33)

Some translations use the word "infidelity" in that blank, giving the connotation of an unfaithful marriage partner. God calls the Wildernites' refusal to put feet to their faith "unfaithfulness." Sadly, what could have been like a long-awaited honeymoon trip turned into forty years of wilderness funerals.

Responding to God's Promises

As Moses gets out his writing utensils and cuneiform tablets to craft the origin story of our first walk-by-faith pioneers, he's writing for a bunch of walk-by-faith dropouts. And strangely, this gives me hope. The very fact that Moses (inspired by God) writes the story of Abram and Sarai with grave digging as background noise means that God's promises aren't voided by our unfaithfulness. The Wildernites might be unfaithful, but they're still the people of the promise. Why? Because *God* is faithful.

Sister, will you respond with faith to this God who lovingly pursues you with his promises? You, too, will be tested. You'll face "Canaanites" of your own. Whose example will you follow?

1. The Wildernites refused to put feet to their faith, even when the promised land was in sight.

What has caused you to "ghost" God?

....

....

....

....

....

How have you responded to tests by turning back?

....

....

....

....

God is still faithful to you. How is he asking you to trust him?

....

....

....

....

2. Abram and Sarai put feet to their faith for a thousand miles.

How is God asking you to have "going without knowing" faith?

....

....

....

....

....

How will you stay where God has led you, even if there are reasons not to?

....

....

....

....

....

....

Faith Is Leaving and Cleaving

I dated a guy for a short time, whom I referred to in my journal as "Mr. Perfect." To me, he seemed like the perfect catch. But for no reason I could explain, I sensed that God was asking me to toss Mr. Perfect back to sea.

"I don't understand, Lord!" I moaned. I decided to put out a "fleece." I knew I'd be seeing Mr. Perfect at a meeting, so I told the Lord, *If he asks me for a date after the meeting, I'll take that as your "thumbs up" on the relationship. But if he doesn't ask me out, I'll walk away.*

It was pretty safe, as fleece exercises go, since we often went out after the meeting. But this time, we talked for an hour in the parking lot—with me wondering the whole time if he was going to ask me out. He didn't.

He drove one way, and I drove the other—then pulled into a parking lot for a good cry. I kept my commitment, though. I was confident this was the Lord's leading, since this was an idea I never would have come up with on my own. As a twenty-something young woman, leaving Mr. Perfect in the rearview mirror was one of my biggest examples yet of putting feet to my faith.

Later, I learned that Mr. Perfect wasn't as perfect as he seemed. While following God doesn't mean bypassing every hardship, this time it did. What a faith-building experience to look back and realize that God had asked me to untangle myself from a relationship that likely would have kept me from other faith ventures. My young step of faith required not only leaving but cleaving to God.

Has God ever prompted an idea that you never would have come up with on your own? Has he ever asked you to leave something (or someone) in the rearview mirror? He often does. This was certainly true for the Abrams.

What three things did God ask Abram to leave behind in Genesis 12:1, and how would this translate for you?

ABRAM'S LIFE	YOUR LIFE
Go from:	
Go from:	
Go from:	

Today, this might translate as, *Delete your social media accounts. Erase all your contacts. Quit your job. Sell your house. Go to the airport and wait for instructions.*

A cross-country move, marrying someone from a different background, or joining a new church denomination might be conceivable to you and me, but not to a Middle Easterner. Even today, family, land, and worship, woven together, form their core identity—and God asked Abram and Sarai to leave it all in the rearview mirror.

Think of what makes up your core identity. What would be hardest to give up and why?

....

....

....

....

....

....

When has God asked you to leave something that you felt defined you?

....

....

....

How does Stephen describe Abram's move in Acts 7:4?

After his father died, God _____ him.

Why might God want to remove Abram and Sarai from their former situation?

....

....

....

What might God want to remove you from, and why?

....

....

....

....

....

Windows from the New Testament

My daughter played water polo in high school. Down in a dark hallway beneath the pool deck was a huge window where you could view the pool underwater. Polo matches are always exciting to watch from the bleachers, but that view into what was happening beneath the surface revealed a whole new level of intensity and struggle. A swimmer might appear to be at a standstill at the surface, but beneath the surface she was straining with all her might.

Stories of faith are like that. There's often an underwater exertion of faith that only God knows about. Genesis gives us more of a "bleacher" view of what happened to Abram and Sarai, but many New Testament passages give us a faith window to discover not only what they did, but why.

Read Hebrews 11:8–10 and 13–16 (we'll return to verses 11–12 later).

What did the Abrams do? Look for verbs and list what was observable from the "bleachers":

....

....

....

....

How many times is the word *faith* used?

....

How is faith described in Hebrews 11:1? How is this required to greet the promised things from afar (v. 13)?

....

....

....

....

Who were "these all" mentioned in Hebrews 11:13? Look back to verses 8–11 (since this refers to recipients of the promise).

Cain	Abraham	Esau
Sarah	Jacob	Isaac

What did they leave (v. 15)? What did they cleave to (v. 16)?

....
....
....
....
....
....

What unique challenges did these things require of Sarai, as a woman?

....
....
....
....
....
....

Leave and Cleave

God consistently calls his people to leave the comfortable and move into the unknown. And this makes sense, if you consider that God is most pleased not by how logical we are, but by how willing we are to be shaped by his promises.

Now, God isn't pleased by foolish craziness. Please don't jump out in traffic to prove that God is with you. But God is glorified when you "leave" whatever he's asked in the rearview mirror and when you "cleave" more tightly to him. That's what the Abrams did. They died, still living in tents, surrounded by Canaanites who were still acting like they owned the place. But to them it was worth it because they believed God had promised them something better.

Living with an Open Parenthesis

promise made

At the end of Abram and Sarai's lives, the promises were still far off—and that's true for us, too. Many of God's promises won't be fulfilled in our lifetime. Can you live with that? Are you okay with God's promises extending past your timeline?

Sarah lived the rest of her life as a stranger. Onlookers probably whispered and pointed, "See that old lady in the tent? It's crazy! She's been there for decades." But Sarai's eyes were fixed on something better—which revealed something to her God.

Take one more look at Hebrews 11:16.

> **But as it is, they desire a better country, that is, a heavenly one. Therefore God is not ashamed to be called their God, for he has prepared for them a city.**

What did they desire? How is it described?

....

....

....

....

....

Put a box around the connector words "therefore" and "for."

Double underline "not ashamed" and draw an arrow to the two reasons (hint: look at the two connector words).

Not Ashamed

Can you imagine hearing that God is not ashamed of you? God was proud to be Abram and Sarai's God. Why? Notice God doesn't say, "I'm not ashamed because they built me a city." No, God is the one building the city. John Piper says, "The reason God is proud to be our God is *not* because *we* have accomplished something so great. But because he has accomplished something great and we *desire* it."[5]

Do you see? Abram and Sarai chose to leave it all in the rearview mirror and cleave to God. They believed his promises. They believed God had something better.

Do you desire "something better" in the life to come? What evidence do you see in your life?

....

....

....

....

What or whom is God asking you to leave in the rearview mirror? How might you cleave to God as "better"?

....

....

....

....

Sister, putting feet to your faith might involve leaving a house, a job, or a whole line of Mr. Perfects in your rearview mirror. But take comfort in this: God sees your beneath-the-surface faith, and he is so proud of you. One day he'll roll out his inheritance and call you home to your eternal promised land, which will be like Eden,[6] only better—and so much better than anything you've left behind.

Below, add your name into the verses that speak of the promised Garden City, where you will dwell:

I also saw the holy city, the new Jerusalem, coming down out of heaven from God, prepared like a bride adorned for her husband.

Then I heard a loud voice from the throne: Look, God's dwelling is with humanity, and he will live with them. _____ will be [among] his peoples, and God himself will be with _____ and will be [her] God. He will wipe away every tear from _____'s eyes.

Death will be no more; grief, crying, and pain will be no more, because the previous things have passed away. (Revelation 21:2–4 csb)

A Stranger Living in a Tent

There are some jewel-studded handprints in the floor of our garage. The hands are child-sized, but according to the etched-in date, those hands now belong to adults. Sometimes when I'm putting away my bike or hanging up garden tools, my eyes fall to that spot and I picture the day young parents pressed little hands into wet cement. I imagine children chattering as they choose embellishing stones and giggling as Rocky's pawprint is included. I picture the wide smiles of grown-ups dreaming about the life they're planning inside this house they're building.

But those plans got cut short. The dreams ended with a realtor's sign. I hope this sweet family went on to live happily somewhere else, but the tiny handprints left in rock-hard cement present a sobering contrast. It's natural to press our hands into the wet cement of this world—hoping for stability and security. But even this world's most beautiful foundations are crumbling and temporary.

A beautiful wedding ring, symbolizing a hollow marriage.

A healthy-looking body, weighed down with cancer and pain.

An ultrasound photo, offering only grief and sorrow.

A closet of dusty clothes, exchanged for hospital gowns.

What has recently reminded you of how temporary and unstable the world is?

....

....

....

....

Abram and Sarai left behind every stable foundation of their lives in search of something better and more permanent.

I'll Show You

Read Genesis 12:4–9.

What do you learn about their entourage?

....

....

....

What did Abram build two of, and how did this demonstrate outwardly something happening to him internally?

....

....

....

Mark the correct reading of Genesis 12:1:

_____"Now the Lord said to Abram, "Go ... to the land that I will show you."

_____"Now the Lord said to Abram, "Go ... to the land that you will be shown."

What amazing thing happened in verse 7, and how was God keeping his promise from Genesis 12:1?

....

....

....

....

When I've traveled to speak in foreign countries where I don't know the language, it's so comforting to have someone meet me at the airport instead of telling me where to go. When Abram arrived in Canaan, God appeared and met him there, just as he had said. Whether or not God appeared to Sarai as well, she must have found it settling to know she was standing on the land God had promised her descendants (Genesis 12:7).

Abram and Sarai's large entourage didn't blend in as they made their way through Canaan—and they weren't quiet about why they were there. Abram built altars and called on God's name (Genesis 12:8), which meant he publicly extolled God,[7] declaring, "This is where God will be worshiped!"

Land-ing Place

You've probably noticed that the promised land is a big part of Abram and Sarai's story, but why? Why the move? Couldn't God have made of them a great nation back in Haran?

What are your initial thoughts?

....

....

....

Nancy Guthrie says, "The Bible is a story of God working out his plan to be at home with his people."[8] The story opens in Genesis and closes in Revelation, with God dwelling among his people—even walking with them.

Picture the evening sun casting shadows from dancing branches across the garden paths of Eden as Adam and Eve stroll with God in the cool of the day (Genesis 3:8). Feel the settled satisfaction of community, peace, flourishing, and belonging—which is encapsulated in the Hebrew word, *shalom*.

When Adam and Eve committed treason against God, they lost access to both God and the garden. The person and the place are inextricably tied in the storyline of the Bible. The Bible is a story of God restoring his people to his presence in that shalom-filled place called heaven.

Consider how leaving a *place* is part of these two stories, and select the words that best characterize each:

	ADAM AND EVE LEAVING EDEN (Genesis 3:14–24)	ABRAM AND SARAI LEAVING HARAN (Hebrews 11:8–10, 13–16)
Obedience or disobedience?		
Anticipation or regret?		
Receiving or losing?		
Coercion or volition?		
Moving toward or away from the better place?		

Divorced from Eden

The Hebrew language is called a poor man's language because there are "less words to go around." See how "poor man" uses a concrete image to create meaning using fewer words? This is how the Hebrew language functions—including here, in this story.

**Genesis 3:24 csb says God
"_____ the man out."**

The Hebrew word here is also often used for "divorce."

Since God often uses marriage to describe his relationship with his people, how does this word demonstrate losing both the person and the place?

....

....

....

What else does God limit their access to in Genesis 3:24? Why?

....

....

....

....

In Christ, you are being restored to the person and place of God. Do you tend to anticipate one more than the other? If so, why?

....

....

....

....

....

Separation and Reconciliation

If you want to know how essential the promised land is to the storyline, imagine a husband and wife who are separated because the wife has been unfaithful. He boards a plane and flies across the country to find her and pursue reconciliation. Her heart melts. They decide to reconcile their marriage. But then the bubble of happiness bursts when the subject of where to live surfaces. The wife doesn't want to leave her new life. She suggests they stay married, but live separately.

Even as I describe this, you can sense how unsatisfying the story would be.

Thankfully, God is not interested in long-distance relationships. From Genesis to Revelation, we see God pursuing us—the unfaithful ones—and working out a plan to restore us to himself, not only relationally but physically. He likes being with us! Even when God divorced Adam and Eve from his presence, it wasn't because he stopped wanting to dwell with his people. And now look at what we see when Abram arrives in Canaan at the oak of Moreh* (Genesis 12:6): God appears. He is once again walking among the trees, making plans to dwell with his people saying, "To your offspring I will give this land" (Genesis 12:7). Doesn't this stir your heart with hope? Doesn't it give you a glimpse at Eden and a taste of shalom? Our God has set a plan in motion to "re-Edenize" the world. Part of belonging to God is anticipating this better place he is preparing for us.

*The oak of Moreh was probably a shrine located in a grove of oak trees where people believed the giant trees evidenced reproductive power. They thought they could worship there and become fertile.[9] Charles Swindoll notes that God was saying in effect, "These people come here to worship gods that do not exist, and they cling to a superstitious hope of becoming fertile. Trust in Me, Abram, and your seed will form a mighty nation."[10]

Tent Pegs

Reread Hebrews 11:8–10 and 13–16.

What parallels do you see between Abram and Sarai's experience and a believer's life today?

What they lived in (v. 9)

....

What they said about themselves and what this clarified (vv. 13–14)

....
....
....

What they *didn't* do to feel "at home" (v. 15)

....
....
....

The better thing they wanted (v. 16) and what was different about it (v. 10)

....
....
....

How does the description in verse 10 remind you of Adam and Eve's home?

....
....
....

I'm not a camper. (I'm not even a glamper.) Nor am I a builder. But even I know that it's best to build your house on a foundation, and pitch your tent on sand, which you can stick a tent peg into.

Tents are temporary; you can pick them up and move. The Bible points to the detail that the Abrams made it to the promised land, but never really settled in. In fact, the only land Abram ever purchased was Sarai's cemetery plot (Genesis 23:20). They lived as "strangers" in tents because they believed God had something better for them. And what was this "something better"? We'd expect the verse to say, "They couldn't wait for better days, when they owned the land like God promised." Instead, it says they looked forward to a different place altogether![11]

From the first time Sarai wiggled her toes in the sand beneath her campsite in Canaan, until the last time she gazed up at the stars twinkling above her tent, there was no evidence of God giving them this promised land. Yet Sarai—along with her husband and their kids after them—"died in faith" (Hebrews 11:13). They chose to build their lives on a foundation you can't stick a tent peg into: the eternal homeland of heaven.

Sister, God hasn't promised you a nation-sized family or land in the Middle East. Those promises were unique to Abram. But the promise of a better home in heaven? That's the promise that creates a foundation for your future.

What does 1 Peter 2:11 say we are to have in common with Sarai?

....

....

What encouragement does 2 Corinthians 4:17–18 give?

....

....

....

Read Ephesians 2:18–20. Who do we have access to? What should we build our lives on?

....

....

....

....

....

....

Listen to more of Heather (and Trina) Cofer's story on Shannon's Live Like It's True *podcast. Go to shannonpopkin.com /promises.*

God's Fullest Display of Faithfulness

Remember Heather Cofer, whose story I shared earlier? Heather told me about an even more catastrophic medical experience that her husband's family—who also served as missionaries in Mongolia—experienced.[12]

Mickey and Trina Cofer hosted a small group of Mongolian villagers each week, teaching them the stories of the Old Testament. Mickey had announced that the following week, he would share about the promised Deliverer who saves from sin and death. That week, however, their son Jonah's horse was spooked by a barking dog while Jonah was riding it. The horse reared and Jonah was thrown, but his foot got caught in the stirrup. The frightened mustang began running wildly—bucking, pounding, and dragging Jonah nearly a hundred yards before the stirrup broke, releasing Jonah's mangled body.

When Trina reached her son's side at the local hospital, she was heartbroken at what she saw.

They later learned that one of the doctors had said, "If that boy lives, their God is the true God."

As her family was airlifted to a larger hospital, Trina softly sang, "Great Is Thy Faithfulness." Forty grueling hours after the accident, they arrived in Korea where Jonah received round-the-clock care during his two-week coma. Then, amazingly, Jonah woke up! It was decided that Trina would take Jonah back to the United States for occupational therapy, and Mickey would return with the other kids to Mongolia to continue their ministry.

The entire village was amazed that the Cofers would return to the place where their son was so badly hurt. That first Sunday after their return, when Mickey shared the gospel, twenty-one people believed and chose to follow Christ. People were baptized and the church was established.

Lifting Your Eyes to the Eternal

If Trina and Mickey were looking for security in the world, they would have returned home for good. Even the Mongolians knew this. But they not only moved to a foreign country, they stayed. Even after something terrifying happened, they stayed put and fixed their gaze on the eternal.

So often we focus on building secure foundations in the here and now. But in this life, we really don't have many tangible promises from God. Some mothers (like Trina) go through tragedy and get their kids back. But there are others who don't. When this happens, does it mean God has been less faithful?

When you are heartbroken over something dreadful or when God doesn't grant the outcome you're begging him for, it's easy to mistake this as his inattentiveness or unfaithfulness to you. But in times like this, you must remember that you're still living in your tent! A day is coming when a new Garden City with unshakable foundations will descend from heaven (Revelation 21:2) and God will make his home on the new earth—a place not only eternal but tangibly real. God will walk with you there among the trees. He'll restore the things you've lost, whether children or home or land (Matthew 19:29). Only in that better homeland will you know just how faithful your God has been.

What experience has been most jarring to your hopes or expectations for the future? How has it helped you lift your gaze to the eternal?

....

....

....

....

Read about John's vision of the Garden City in Revelation 21:1-4. Rephrase what the voice from heaven says as "I will" statements from God:

....

....

....

How can you respond to these in faith, the way Abram and Sarai did?

....

....

....

What does Revelation 21:14 say there will be twelve of, and what does this mean for you?

....

....

....

Faith is believing God when he promises you a homeland with a foundation that will never crumble. As you read the verses below, insert your name and picture yourself pressing your handprint into the wet cement of your heavenly dwelling where your future is secure.

_____ will say to the Lord, "My refuge and

my fortress, my God, in whom I trust." . . .

Because _____ has made the Lord her dwell-

ing place—the Most High, who is her refuge—

no evil shall be allowed to befall _____,

   no plague come near _____'s tent.

(Psalm 91:2, 9–10)

Consider Him Faithful

Sarai lived her whole life being shaped by a set of promises that she never got to see come true. And yet, here's our theme verse for this study:

> [Sarai] considered him faithful who had promised. (Hebrews 11:11)

Who made the promises? God did. Who kept the promises? God did. At the end, when Sarai looked back and considered the God making his promises to her—when she thought carefully and examined all she knew about him—she saw him as faithful.

We "consider him faithful" in the same way. We gather up information about what has happened in that long stretch between the parentheses. Remember, faithfulness is only demonstrated over time. And we have the advantage of experiencing God's faithfulness—not just as it overlaps with our own timelines, but as it extends over the centuries of God's history with his people.

promise made   promise kept

Retell, Reflect, Rehearse

In each week of our study, lesson 5 will offer you the opportunity to:

RETELL: God didn't give us a theology book; he gave us stories. In this section, you'll summarize part of Sarai's story, particularly through her eyes. Think of each story like a velvet pouch, full of gems about God and his promises. The story is what holds it all together. So by the end of this study, you'll have six velvet pouches lined up on a shelf in your mind—ready to retrieve for yourself and share with others.

REFLECT: We don't just want to know Sarai's story, we want to be shaped by it. In this section, I'll ask you to reflect on what God was showing you in the previous four lessons and then invite you to respond.

REHEARSE: In this section, I'll ask you to select a promise from God and, like Sarai, "consider him faithful who promised" (see Hebrews 11:11).

Ready to give it a try?

RETELL

Summarize the story of God calling Abram and Sarai to the promised land. Read Genesis 12:1–7; Hebrews 11:8–10, 13–16.

I will, I will, I will ...

....

....

....

....

....

....

Leaving and cleaving / Going without knowing

....

....

....

A blessing testing

....

....

....

Living in tents, seeking a homeland

....

....

....

REFLECT

Review some key points from the week and reflect on how God is inviting you to respond.

When God told Abram and Sarai to move to Canaan, they not only obeyed, they stayed. They not only left home, they didn't return home. They practiced faith not just with their heads, but also with their feet.

Faith is going without knowing. How is God asking you to put feet to your faith? How is he asking you to step into the unknown?

....

....

....

....

Faith is leaving and cleaving. What is God asking you to put or *leave* in the rearview mirror?

....

....

....

How is God asking you to—by faith—stay put and not turn back?

....

....

Even with the promised land in sight, the Wildernites wanted to ghost God and go back. But even though God called them "unfaithful," they were still the people of the promise. Why? Because God is faithful.

How have you been one of the "unfaithful" ones? How does God's unrelenting faithfulness surprise you?

....

....

....

Have you been ghosting God in a time of fear or testing? How is he asking you to repent?

....

....

....

God's promises create a foundation for your future. If your world is currently crumbling, don't presume that God has been unfaithful. Remember: You're still living in your tent, which is temporary! Only in that shalom-filled Garden City, which is both eternal and tangible, will you know just how faithful God has been.

What is something you've lost? Is it listed in Matthew 19:29? What real and tangible things do you believe God will restore to you in heaven?

....

....

....

....

What are some "crumbling foundations" you've experienced in life? How can you make God's promises of heaven the foundation for your future?

....

....

....

....

....

REHEARSE

The story of the Bible begins with God dwelling with his people and ends with God dwelling with his people. This is the part of the story where God begins to unveil his plan to re-Edenize the world—and it all starts with a set of promises to a particular family God chooses to bless.

In this part of Sarai's story, what have you learned about the God who says, "I will," and who makes and keeps his promises?

....

....

....

....

Will you be shaped by God's promises? Choose a meaningful promise from page 291, along with a verse to memorize. Write them both below.

....

....

....

....

....

....

....

....

....

Betrayal
and Rescue

Betrayal and Rescue

Say You're My Sister

I called my mom after a trip to the grocery store during the COVID-19 pandemic and said, "The shelves were completely empty! It looked so strange!" Perhaps, like me, you had never experienced a store with empty shelves or shortages on everyday items like toilet paper or yeast. And yet, I made it through a global pandemic without missing a meal—which means I haven't come close to experiencing what the Abrams faced in this part of their story.

The Abrams have encountered two surprising details since arriving in the promised land.

　　1. What is in Canaan (Genesis 12:6)?

....

....

....

　　2. What is not in Canaan (Genesis 12:10)?

....

....

....

If you faced a shortage emergency, list the places or people you could turn to for help. Circle any that you think might have been available to the Abrams, while living in Canaan.

....

....

....

What was Abram's plan (Genesis 12:10)?

....

....

....

....

Mark the movement noted in verse 10 on your map on page 18.

The Abrams have pitched their tent in the promised land, but the Blessing Bus has not only failed to arrive, it seems to be backing up into the next time zone for the foreseeable future.

Why would God send them into a drought? They're strangers here, with no friends. Aliens with no rights. Herders with no water. As the promises seem to dry up instead of materialize, the Abrams pull up their tent pegs in one foreign country and head to the next.

Crossing into Egypt

Some people criticize anyone in the Bible who heads for Egypt, yet it only takes a glance at a map of the Nile River delta to make Egypt an obvious choice during a drought. Also, since God told Mary and Joseph to flee and take baby Jesus to Egypt (Matthew 2:13), apparently it was *sometimes* the right choice. I'm not sure we should criticize Abram for leading his crew to Egypt. I *do* think we should think critically about his plan for crossing the border.

I didn't realize until I visited Egypt a few years back that the pyramids were built about five hundred years before the Abrams' arrival.[1] (You might want to draw some pyramids on your map.) Historians are still baffled at how they were constructed. My husband was baffled at how Pharaoh thought he was going to escape his sarcophagus in the afterlife. One thing is sure: those pyramids are impressive. As Abram traveled with his thirsty entourage of people and animals toward Egypt, it was probably quite intimidating.

Now, when an author (in this case, Moses) uses dialogue, we should listen very carefully, for "out of the abundance of the heart his mouth speaks" (Luke 6:45). Abram's words give us insight into what he's been mulling over:

> **When he was about to enter Egypt, he said to Sarai his wife,**
>
> **"I know that you are a woman beautiful in appearance, and**
>
> **when the Egyptians see you, they will say, 'This is his wife.'**
>
> **Then they will kill me, but they will let you live. Say you are**
>
> **my sister, that it may go well with me because of you, and**
>
> **that my life may be spared for your sake." (Genesis 12:11–13)**

In the verses above:
- **Put a box around the words "know," "will," or "may."**
- **Above each pronoun, write who is being referred to.**

What does Abram predict will happen and what is this prediction based on?

....

....

....

....

What is Abram's plan and how does it indicate or not indicate faith?

....

....

....

....

How is verse 12 inconsistent with any of God's promises in Genesis 12:2-3?

....

....

....

Abram knows two things: he knows that Sarai is beautiful, and he knows what people are like. People are greedy and self-serving. People will kill a man, just to get his wife. Yet consider the irony:

Who does Abram want it to go well with (v. 13)?

....

....

....

Whose safety is jeopardized? (Look ahead to verse 15.)

....

....

How are husbands to treat their wives according to the following verses?

    Ephesians 5:25 ....

....

....

1 Peter 3:7 ....

....

....

"She's My W-ister"

Abram is entering Egypt as a wealthy foreigner seeking asylum, and he knows his stay there won't be free. He's worried, though, that the first thing they'll want is his unusually beautiful wife—and Abram is not wrong.

If you're wondering why Sarai went along with Abram's "Sister Act," think again. Without Abram shielding her, she would be vulnerable to *anyone* who wanted to take her. Sarai needed Abram. And he was saying he needed *her* to lie and play along.

It sounds a bit like emotional blackmail and it's not a noble plan, but it might not be as self-serving as it first appears.

Read Genesis 29:18–20 about Jacob (Abram and Sarai's grandson). Record any implied details you can find about bride bartering:

....

....

....

....

....

Bride bartering was customary in this part of the world. And as you just read, negotiations could stretch out over years—just like famines. With that in mind, it's possible Abram was trying to buy time.[2] He had cleverly come up with a way for suitors to come *to* him, not *through* him to get to Sarai. Perhaps an Egyptian would say, "I'll give you five camels for your sister." And Abram could say, "You think she's a five-camel woman? Look at her! She's worth at least ten."

But here's what Abram didn't take into consideration: Pharaoh doesn't barter; he just takes what he wants. We'll see that in the next lesson.

Threats or Theology

For now, let's think about what Abram was thinking about on his way to Egypt. Because we, too, need to think about what we're thinking.

Which was Abram more focused on?

His Threats   **His Theology**

Is Abram being shaped by God's promises? Why or why not?

....

....

....

....

....

It's not wrong to protect ourselves against threats. It's not wrong to make *plans* to protect ourselves against threats. But if we're to be shaped by God's promises, we can't be consumed with the threats and completely forget our theology.

Theology, by the way, is just a fancy word for the study of God. At this point, Abram honestly doesn't know much about God. Now, Abram can't open his Bible, the way you can. He can't flip back and forth between God's promises made and kept the way we can. He only has promises at this point, not fulfillments.

But think about the Wildernites, hearing this story. The Wildernites know how things are going to turn out. They are living proof of God's faithfulness. The fact that they are a free nation means that God is going to keep his promise to protect Abram and Sarai from enemies (Genesis 12:3) and to make their family of two into a great nation (Genesis 12:2).

From the Wildernites' vantage point, which of Abram's fears in Egypt (listed below) are logically impossible and why?

☐ **Abram is afraid of starving from severe famine.**

☐ **Abram is afraid the Egyptians will treat him with contempt.**

☐ **Abram is afraid of being murdered.**

....

....

....

....

To be shaped by God's promises, we start with what we know about God and consider what God has promised. Then we make logical conclusions and act accordingly.

By Faith or by Fear?

Again, Abram doesn't have a Bible tucked under his arm as he enters Egypt and passes those intimidating pyramids. He's just beginning to learn what God is like, so we can certainly empathize as Abram's words betray what he's been thinking about. Abram hasn't been calling to mind God's promises or reflecting on what God was like the day he appeared (Genesis 12:7). Abram has been thinking about what people are like. He's been fretting about what these vicious Egyptians might do! Abram may have been calling on God's name and walking by faith back in Canaan but as he enters Egypt, Abram is walking by fear. It's only natural to be consumed with the threats. It's supernatural, however, to be consumed with your theology.

Perhaps, like Abram, you've been doing what comes naturally in this dangerous world filled with selfish people: you've been completely consumed with the threats. Yet armed with a thick Bible that tells you what God is like, you have the option of walking by faith, not fear. To start, you must think about what you're thinking. Will you focus on what people are like or what God is like? Each new threat offers you a new opportunity to steady your heart with your theology. Let's take a moment and practice.

LIVING BY FEAR List out the threats you regularly think about, either globally, locally, or personally. How are you tempted to fear because of what people are like?	LIVING BY FAITH List something you know about God's character or promises in response to each threat. (Turn to page 291 if you need help.) How are you steadied by thinking about what God is like?

Remember this:

It's natural to say, "I know what people are like."

It's supernatural to say, "I know what God is like."

Which will you allow to consume your thoughts today?

Taken

Early in our marriage, Ken and I were walking out to the parking lot after church one cold, wintry day. The pavement was icy, the wind was blowing, and Ken was focused on getting to the car as quickly as possible. I wasn't wearing the right shoes and was trying not to slip walking down the steps, so I was about ten paces behind Ken—and feeling rather abandoned.

That's when our pastor spotted the scenario while driving through the parking lot and called out with some wise counsel to my new husband: "Come on, man! Go help your wife!" The fact that I can still remember this twenty-five years later speaks to how validated I felt in that moment. (Thanks, Pastor Chip.) But Ken seems downright chivalrous compared to Sarai's husband in this story.

Read Genesis 12:11–15.

How was Abram's concern proven to be valid?

....

....

....

What happened that he didn't count on?

....

....

....

How did Abram put each of the following at risk?

Sarai ....

....

Their marriage ....

....

God's plan to bless them ....

....

....

Sarai is silent in this section. What might she be thinking or feeling?

....

....

....

How old is Sarai at this point? Check your timeline on page 17.

....

Pharaoh's New Wife

Let the gravity of this word fall like a rock in your gut:

And the woman was _____. (Genesis 12:15)

Circle the reference to Sarai in this verse. She has become a nameless, unmarried woman in a foreign country who now belongs to the most powerful man.

You might wonder how at this age, Sarai could be at risk for human trafficking (which this basically is). Abram and Sarai lived about twice as long as people today, so perhaps they aged at half the speed.[3] Regardless, Abram knew his wife was beautiful. He was worried it would cause problems, and it did.

In the previous lesson, we said Abram was possibly counting on bride bartering to buy himself some time. Yet, Pharaoh didn't barter. Pharaoh just took. Take another look at the timing details we're given:

Who sees Sarai in Genesis 12:14?

....

Who is talking about Sarai in Genesis 12:15? Who are they talking to?

....

....

What happened next (v. 15)?

....

....

....

How much time do you suppose passed between these instances?

....

I have no answer to that last question, but here's what I want Abram to do in that moment after Pharaoh's princes leave: I want him to hero up, ditch the Sister Act, and say, "Babe, whatever happens, I'm not gonna let them take you." Instead, Abram cowardly sticks with his plan, which puts his wife in a morally compromising situation. Rather than protecting Sarai's purity and honor, Abram protects himself. He chooses to walk by fear, not faith.

Fear and faith lead in opposite directions; you can't walk both ways at once. When Pharaoh's princes return to collect "the woman," Abram remains silent. In fear, he lets them take his wife.

Friend, if this grieves and sickens you, I think you've got the right idea of the scene.

Read Ephesians 5:25–33.

Who are husbands to emulate, and how?

....

....

....

....

What is Christ's priority for his bride in verse 26? How is Abram deprioritizing this for Sarai?

....

....

....

....

How is marriage a metaphor for something else (vv. 25, 32)?

....

....

....

....

....

The Marriage Metaphor

A wife being protected by her husband is embedded into the core of the Bible's story. When God gives Eve to Adam in Genesis 2, marriage itself is presented as a valuable gift. Marriage is real. But from the beginning, God intended marriage also as a metaphor to point to something even more precious.

Think of a wedding ring. If my husband trades his ring for some gloves on a cold day, he not only disrespects the ring by treating it like a trinket; he also disrespects me. See how the ring represents something more?

Marriage is the same way. Marriage is meant to shed light on the climax of the whole Bible—that moment when Christ laid down his life for his Bride. In a world without marriage, how could we possibly understand the significance of this moment? Marriage—with the picture of a man laying down his life for his bride, is precious to the story of the Bible. And the image is cheapened when a husband protects himself and puts his wife at risk.

We see this in faithless Abram.

Have you known any protective, self-sacrificing husbands and fathers? Has faith contributed to their character?

....

....

....

....

Have you known any self-serving men who put their wives and daughters at risk? Has fear contributed to their character?

....

....

....

For Richer, for Poorer

I like stories where the good guy gets rewarded and the bad guy gets what's coming to him. That's why this next part of our story is so disorienting. While Sarai is detained in Pharaoh's harem—unprotected by Abram or by the status of her marriage, look what's happening to Abram.

Read Genesis 12:16.

Who is being treated well, and for whose sake?

....

....

....

List out the gifts:

....

....

....

Can you think of any modern examples of one person benefitting from another person being taken?

....

....

....

Fill in the blanks:

Sarai was _____ beautiful. (Genesis 12:14)

Abram was _____ rich. (Genesis 13:2)

Rehearse these details from week 1:

Who said, "I will"?

....

Who "walked the aisle between the pieces" and what did this mean?

....

....

....

Which promise is God keeping as Abram gets rich? (See Genesis 12:2.)

....

....

....

This is hard for me. I have no problem with Abram getting rich, especially since God promised this (Genesis 12:2). But for him to get rich just after he's put his wife at risk to save his own skin? *That* makes no sense. The timing just doesn't sit right with me—and my displeasure reveals something about my theology.

I want God to bless and honor people who do what's right. And yet, the Bible is not a story about people getting what they deserve from God. It's a story about people getting what they *don't* deserve. Case in point: Abram. As I watch him receive wealth at Sarai's expense, I so desperately want to categorize Abram as "that sinner over there." But if there's a "righteous over here" group, I don't belong in it—which is why this story's theology lesson is such good news.

God is not keeping his promises because of Abram's faithfulness; God is keeping his promises because of *God's* faithfulness. This is one of the most important and counterintuitive truths proclaimed in this story and in the broader storyline of the Bible. Just like with Abram, God does not bless us because we are faithful and good; God blesses us because *he* is faithful and good.

Do you deserve God's blessings? Why or why not?

....

....

....

....

....

What does Romans 3:10–12 say about this?

....

....

....

How is this story about Abram an example of 2 Timothy 2:13?

....

....

....

....

Out of Her Control

So God is being faithful to Abram, but what about Sarai? She has no control over this situation. She can't control the famine. She can't control Abram. She can't control Pharaoh. She can't control the outcome. Can you imagine the crushing fear, insecurity, and (undeserved) shame she's likely dealing with?

Perhaps you can relate. Is there someone who should have protected you and didn't? Worse yet, is that person prospering while you suffer? Maybe your mom turned a blind eye to the abuse. Your dad stayed quiet after a family member did the unthinkable. Your church or your boss didn't believe your story.

Sister, if you have endured something like this, may I speak softly into your soul? Abuse is wretched. Self-serving passivity is evil. And if you are sorting through a situation past or present that has been personally costly and painful, I hope you'll avail yourself of every measure of protection, safety, and support available to you. And yet the quest to take and get and keep control—as promising as it seems—won't ultimately satisfy you. Clamping down white knuckles won't bring the peace and security you long for; only God can do that.

When we are forced to recognize we're not in control, we're positioned to realize that God *is*. As the story unfolds, we're going to see that Sarai was never forgotten or abandoned by God; but let's not rush to the resolution. Let's linger with Sarai in those (likely) months when God allowed her to face the disparity between his promises and her situation. From Sarai's perspective, there was no second parenthesis in sight.

promise made

Why does God allow these long stretches between the parentheses, when a month can feel like a year and a year can feel like a century? We aren't told explicitly, but we do see a pattern in our Bibles. In the thousands of years between Genesis 3 when God first promised Jesus and Matthew 1 when he sent him, a particular truth is amplified: God keeps his promises. This expansive gap between the parentheses displays something that a thinner Bible couldn't: God is faithful to his people. Even after thousands of years, he doesn't forget his promises.

From Sarai's immediate perspective, it would seem that God *has* forgotten his promises. Either that or he cannot keep them. But faithfulness, remember, is only demonstrated over time. Over time, we'll see that God can and will keep his promises. Nothing is out of his control. But for now, Sarai is invited to "cling in between" the parentheses by faith.

What out-of-control situation are you experiencing? How has it cost you?

....

....

....

Who else may be prospering while you suffer?

....

....

....

How has this situation proven to you that you are not in control?

....

....

....

How has your quest for control been unsatisfying?

....

....

....

What have you learned in that gap between the parentheses that you otherwise wouldn't have?

....

....

....

....

Sana's Story

When Sana was four years old she was placed in foster care, but it wasn't until much later that she discovered why: her mother had been selling her to men for drugs.

Her *mother*. The one who was supposed to keep her safe had exploited her. It's stories like Sana's that cause us to ask, "Where was God? Why did he let this happen?" But amazingly, Sana looks back and sees

God keeping her safe. The foster home Sana entered was hosting a church in their basement, and that's where Sana met Jesus.

As a little girl, Sana remembers clinging to God's promise that she was safe—even when she didn't feel safe. Sure, she doubted and questioned sometimes. But even in her darkest moments (like being molested in respite care), Sana sensed God's presence. She knew she was not alone.

Some might look at Sana's story and see evidences of God's *un*faithfulness. Like Sarai, she was exploited. Like Sarai, she felt abandoned. Like Sarai, there was a discrepancy between what God promised and what she experienced—at least for a time. But Sana looks back on all these hardships and says, "I wasn't buried, I was planted." It's not the story she would have chosen, but it's the story God wrote for her. And this story has given her credibility for her current ministry—pointing others who have endured similar hardships to Christ.

All along, God had a purpose for Sana. He had a story of his own faithfulness he was telling. The same was true of Sarai—and the same is true of you!

Listen to more of Sana's story on Shannon's Live Like It's True podcast. Go to shannonpopkin.com /promises.

Blessing and Cursing

When "COVID" became a household word, we all got a better sense of what a "plague" is. It's different from the flu. It lasts longer than a weekend, and spreads farther than your house. It affects your life in a big way. All of these are things Sarai is experiencing in Pharaoh's harem.

Read Genesis 12:17.

Who has been afflicted? By whom? Who is referenced as the cause?

....

....

....

Who is being revealed as the most powerful and how?

....

....

....

The first word, *but*, signals contrast. Who is being contrasted and how?

....

....

....

Who caused this?

....

....

We might answer that last question in several ways. Pharaoh is definitely not the good guy in the story. Like the other pharaohs of Egypt, he likely thought of himself as a god to be worshiped, and he certainly felt entitled to whatever woman he wanted to take. But then, we were never expecting Pharaoh to be a blessing. Yet that *is* what we expected from Abram.

Callous Abram

God's first words to Abram are so foundational—which is why I keep referring you back to them. Remember that the Hebrew word for "blessed" connotes wealth and well-being. God says,

> I will _____ you and make your name great, so that
>
> you will be a _____. (Genesis 12:2)

How has the first part come true?

....

....

What would the others in this story say about the last part?

....

....

....

Pharaoh's household has been hit with not one, but multiple plagues. People are suffering—probably for months, if not years. Yet Abram is callous enough to walk past their pain, saying, "Hey, sis!" It's likely that the plagues stopped at Sarai's door (which may be how Pharaoh identified her as the source). But that doesn't mean Sarai is in the harem having a picnic. She's surrounded by stressed, sick, or grieving people who are not only strangers but from a culture foreign to her. No doubt she feels betrayed and abandoned by Abram.

Abram, the Chieftain

There's one more thing that Sarai knows about Abram that you might not yet know. Flip forward a couple of chapters and look at what happens when someone else from Abram's family is taken—this time as a prisoner of war, outside Egypt.

Read Genesis 14:12–16.

Who was taken and why?

....

....

....

List any details given or implied about Abram's resources and capabilities.

....

....

....

If I were the director of a movie called *Abram*, this would be my opening scene. The camera would zoom in on Abram springing into action after receiving word that his nephew had been taken. We'd see his 318 men mounted on horses, ready to launch a two-pronged attack in the night—and there, leading the charge would be Abram, winning our admiration and respect.

My goal would be to erase any imagery from your Sunday School flannelgraph of an old man with a beard and a cane, slogging through the desert with his pretty wife and a donkey. No, Abram is loyal, brave, and resourced. He's a war hero! A chieftain. When we take this information back to our story at hand, I'm wondering why our valiant hero isn't doing something to rescue his damsel in distress. I'll bet Sarai was wondering the same thing.

Struck by the Lord

Look back at your answer in the first set of questions regarding who caused this situation.

Compare your answer with what is said in Genesis 12:17.

....

....

Reread Genesis 12:1–3.

God promised to curse anyone who does what?

....

....

....

How is God keeping his promise, and to whom?

....

....

....

....

A God Who Curses

God keeps two types of promises: to bless and to curse. Just a quick scroll through social media will reveal how much we Christians embrace God's promises to bless. But have you seen any memes lately about God's promises to curse? Yet both are true. God promises to bless *and* curse.

Take a step back and think of the Bible's main storyline. In the opening scenes, we see God pouring out his *blessing* on Adam and Eve, who immediately side with the serpent and sin against God. This triggers consequences and *curses*.

Who did God curse in Genesis 3:14, and why was this good news for Adam, Eve, and us?

....

....

....

Who will be enemies, according to Genesis 3:15? Whose offspring is mentioned?

....

....

....

....

....

When God drew up enemy lines, the deceiving serpent was on one side and Adam and Eve were on the other. They probably gasped with relief when they realized God was siding *with* them. If he had left them over on the enemy's side, they would have been stuck with no way to heal from sin, sickness, or death, and no way to eradicate evil. But God put himself on their side. He cursed the true enemy and promised the woman's offspring would one day crush him for good. Who then is this offspring?

This is the question. As we turn the pages of Genesis, the search narrows as God commits himself to Abram and his (coming soon) family. *Aha!* we say. Could this be the family line from which the snake-crushing Savior will come?

But it's not until Matthew 1 that this promised offspring, Jesus, enters the story. And when he does, God's battle lines are intact. God sides with and promises to bless those who side with Jesus Christ. And God promises to curse those who side with the serpent and reject Christ.

What do the following verses say about God's enemies?

Matthew 25:41, 46 ....

....

John 3:36 ....

....

2 Peter 2:4, 9 ....

....

Revelation 20:10 ....

....

Have you sided with Jesus Christ? If so, what curses will you avoid?

....

....

....

....

Protecting the Promised One

Perhaps you haven't thought to rejoice in God's promises to curse the serpent, but you should. This ancient enemy has been trying to wipe out your only hope from day one. Have you noticed—only a few verses in to the Abrams' story, how many ways this family line is at risk of dying out? First Abram and Sarai experience infertility issues, then famine, then the risk of wife-snatching murderers. And now their marriage has split up, and Sarai is in another man's bedroom.

How is Sarai's future offspring at risk in Genesis 12:15?

....

....

....

How is God's promise to curse (Genesis 12:3) designed to protect Sarai's future offspring, Jesus?

....

....

Do you have any new insights on how God is keeping his promises in Genesis 12:17?

....

....

....

....

....

As the readers of God's great story, we should be wringing our hands when Sarai is taken. Without Sarai and Abram's promised offspring, there is no one to crush the serpent and eradicate the evil and suffering that we all live under.

And though Sarai's husband never comes to the rescue, God does. He rescues her by keeping his promise—not to bless, but to curse. Back when God said he would curse anyone who treated the Abrams with contempt (Genesis 12:3), he wasn't just saying, "I got your back." Yes, God promised to protect them. Yet far more than their safety was at stake. This plague would ultimately protect the family line from which Jesus would come.

Why did Sarai—trapped in Pharaoh's harem—ultimately have nothing to fear?

....

....

....

....

Your Rescue

I wish I could point to this story in the Bible and promise that—like Sarai—you too will be rescued from every harmful situation in the world, but that would be misleading. You read Sana's story in the last lesson. You have your own stories of people who love Jesus yet get hurt by evil people. We live in a dangerously corrupt world, and we can't assume that since God ultimately rescued Sarai, it's fine to leave our doors unlocked at night.

The promises we've been referring back to in Genesis 12 were unique to Abram and Sarai. And yet, their story is linked to ours, remember? I don't think it's a stretch to say that when God rescued Sarai, he was also thinking of you. He was thinking of every one of us who needed our rescuer, Jesus Christ, to be born into Sarai's family line.

Jesus knew all about what people are like—how greedy and self-serving we all are. And yet, when Jesus anticipated the cross, he wasn't consumed with what people are like; he was consumed with what God is like! Jesus chose to focus not on the threats, but on his theology. Jesus laid down his life because he knew God would raise it up (Romans 8:11).

Do you see the contrast? Those who don't see how the promises could possibly come true are cowardly and self-serving. Like Abram, they put other people at risk. But those who live like the promises *are* true—believing that God is on their side—become like Jesus, filled with bravery, self-sacrifice, and trust in God.

How has focusing on the threats caused you to be cowardly and self-serving?

....

....

....

....

Have you put others at risk out of fear?

....

....

....

....

....

What difference would it make if you focused on what you know about God, rather than what you know about people?

....

....

....

....

....

....

....

....

A Mini Exodus

We're not sure how, but Pharaoh found out the secret Abram was keeping. Perhaps Sarai didn't catch whatever was going around and Pharaoh traced the plagues to her. Whatever the case, Pharaoh learned that Sarai was Abram's wife, not his sister.

Read Genesis 12:18–20.

How does Pharaoh give the impression he is personally offended?

....

....

What does Abram say? Why do you suppose this is?

....

....

....

How many times is the word "wife" mentioned? What does this emphasize?

....

....

Who is correcting whom? Why is this ironic?

....

....

....

In this story, who do Abram and Pharaoh each see as powerful? Who is correct?

....

....

....

What two things did Abram leave Egypt with (v. 20) and how is God keeping his promises?

....

....

....

....

Read Genesis 13:1-4 and mark your map on page 18 with Abram's movement.

Picture Abram and Sarai passing those same pyramids on their way out of Egypt. On the way there, Abram had been consumed with the threats. He had been saying, "I know what people are like." But on the way out of Egypt, don't you think he must have been consumed with his theology? Look how God had just shown them what he is like!

Sarai was taken by the most powerful man in the land. And yet Pharaoh wasn't in control; God was! Pharaoh wasn't to be feared; God was. This is a powerful display of God keeping his promises. And as a result, Abram and Sarai get their own little personal exodus—based on God's faithfulness, not their own.

Unmistakable Parallels

I read an article in 2021 about the Spanish Flu of 1918. The article explained that the virus had affected a third of the population. It hit in waves, and they tried to stop the spread with quarantining. As I read, I was nodding along, saying, "Yep. That all sounds very familiar." Now, if I had read that same article the year *before* COVID struck, it would have seemed irrelevant. But because I had just lived through something comparable, the similarities were easy to spot.

Seat yourself among the Wildernites. Remember their backstory? They, too, were trapped in Egypt under a powerful Pharaoh. And they too experienced God's deliverance. Keep in mind that there's a five-hundred-year lapse between these two stories. Note below any similarities you find.

THE ABRAMS	THE WILDERNITES	SHARED EXPERIENCE
Genesis 12:10	Genesis 45:11	
Genesis 12:16	Exodus 3:22; 12:35	
Genesis 12:17	Exodus 9:14	
Genesis 12:20	Exodus 12:31	

How does each story teach about God's faithfulness?

....

....

....

....

....

How did the two Pharaohs react differently, but with the same result? How was this evidence of God keeping his promises?

....

....

....

....

Think of the Wildernites hearing this story. What threats are they facing? (See Numbers 14 if you need a refresher.) How might Abram's negative example of focusing on the threats challenge them to focus on their theology?

....

....

....

....

....

....

The Theology of Moses's Parents

Look at one more interesting parallel. Do you remember what happened to Moses, the leader of the Wildernites, when he was a baby? Pharaoh—who was worried about being outnumbered by the Israelites—commanded that all of their newborn baby boys be thrown into the Nile. But Moses's parents hid him in a basket, floating in the Nile, where Pharaoh's daughter found and adopted him. (You can read the story in Exodus 2.)

Do you see the similarity between Moses and Sarai? They were both taken into Pharaoh's household. Let's look at one similarity and one difference in their stories.

Read Hebrews 11:23. What did Moses's parents notice about him?

....

....

What did Abram say he knew about Sarai (Genesis 12:11)?

....

....

How did Moses's parents respond to the threat of their Pharaoh? See Hebrews 11:23.

....

....

Circle the first two words of this verse and fill in the blanks:

> **By faith ... [Moses's parents] were _____ _____.**
> **(Hebrews 11:23)**

Does this verse mean that Moses's parents had no fear? I think not. Their baby was at risk of being found and thrown into the Nile. But they didn't live by fear. They lived by faith—and that faith made all the difference.

Look at the contrast: Abram lived by fear. He said, "I know what people are like." Abram was cowardly and self-serving. He betrayed his wife instead of protecting her.

But Moses's parents lived by faith. They knew what Pharaoh was like, but with their actions, they said, "I also know what *God* is like." They were honorable and brave. They defied Pharaoh and protected their baby.

Responding to Your Pharaoh

Sister, there will always be threats. There will always be another "Pharaoh" who seems to have control. But you get to choose whether you're consumed with the threats or your theology.

What threat are you currently facing?

- Is there another woman who has your husband's attention?
- Is your child addicted to porn or drugs?
- Is your daughter-in-law threatening to keep you from your grandkids?
- Is your child struggling with gender dysphoria?
- Is there a world news story that has you tied in knots?

Who is the "Pharaoh" in your story? What threat do you face?

....

....

....

....

It's natural to live by fear. It's supernatural to live by faith. You get to choose: Will you respond like Abram? Or will you be like Moses's parents, who, "By faith . . . were not afraid" (Hebrews 11:23)? Write your name in the blank:

By faith _____ was not afraid.

What would it look like to live like this is true? Write a prayer to God, asking for supernatural faith, bravery, and fearlessness.

....

....

....

....

....

....

....

Considering Him Faithful

Sarai lived through a completely out-of-control situation. She was a foreigner, a woman with no rights, and she was taken into the harem of the most powerful man of the land. Things looked beyond awful, and yet God was faithful.

RETELL

Summarize the story of Abram and Sarai in Egypt, and include these three quotes:

"Say you are my sister." (Genesis 12:13)

"The woman was taken." (Genesis 12:15)

"What is this you have done to me?" (Genesis 12:18)

....

....

....

....

....

....

....

....

....

....

REFLECT

Review some key points from the week and reflect on how God is inviting you to respond.

Abram focused on what people are like, and his fear made him forget what God is like. It's natural to focus on the threats; it's supernatural to focus on your theology. Like Abram, we have the choice to live by faith or by fear.

What threatening person or situation have you been consumed with? What truth about God are you forgetting?

....

....

....

....

....

Make a plan. How will you focus on what God is like the next time you're tempted to focus on what people are like? How will you choose faith, not fear?

....

....

....

....

....

It was disorienting to see Abram get rich at Sarai's expense. But the Bible is not a story about people who do it all right and get what they deserve; it's a story about people who do it all wrong and get what they don't deserve—like Abram did. And all along, Sarai was never abandoned or forgotten by God.

How has it been disorienting to watch someone else benefit while you suffer? How does Sarai's story remind you that God has not forgotten or abandoned you?

....

....

....

....

....

Why is it good news for you that the Bible is not about people getting what they deserve, but rather getting the blessings they _don't_ deserve?

....

....

....

....

....

In what situation is God asking you to trust him for the peace and security that white-knuckled control can never bring you?

....

....

....

....

....

For (likely) months, Sarai was faced with the disparity between God's promises and her current situation in Pharaoh's palace. Yet while she was there, Sarai was positioned to see that she was not in control, but God was.

What situation is God using to show you that you're not in control? How has he used this to position you to see that he is?

....

....

....

....

What is God teaching you in the gap between the parentheses, which you wouldn't have otherwise learned?

....

....

....

....

In response to the threat Pharaoh posed, Abram lived by fear and was cowardly and self-serving. Moses's parents lived by faith and were brave and selfless.

How is God asking you to respond to your "Pharaoh" by faith?

....

....

....

....

What is one way that—by faith—you will be brave and selfless?

....

....

....

....

....

REHEARSE

In this part of the story, God used plagues in Pharaoh's household to protect and rescue Sarai along with her coming offspring, Jesus—who is our only hope of being rescued from sin.

How do you see God demonstrating his faithfulness by keeping his promises in this part of Sarai's story?

....

....

....

....

....

Will you be shaped by God's promises? Choose one of the "Here and Now: Promises of Spiritual Life and Refreshment" from page 292, along with a verse to memorize. Write them both below.

....

....

....

....

....

....

....

....

....

....

Shame and Control

Shame and Control

The Brittle Branch on the Family Tree

Years ago, we had a tree in our front yard that was leafy and green except for a huge, leafless, brittle branch that stuck out on one side. It was an eyesore. It didn't provide shade or aesthetic appeal. No matter what we tried, it didn't grow leaves, so I'm sure you can imagine the limb's ill-fated demise.

In our story, Sarai is introduced as the brittle branch sticking out of the most important family tree in the history of the world.

God Alone

Back in Genesis 15 (we briefly touched down here in our very first lesson), we saw God walk the aisle through the pieces and commit to the covenant he was making with Abram. But before this covenant ceremony, God had a conversation with Abram, assuring him of what exactly God was promising.

Read Genesis 15:1–6.

What assumption has Abram made which God corrects (vv. 2–4)?

....

....

....

What action and imagery does God use to reiterate what he has promised (v. 5)?

....

....

....

According to verse 6, what was Abram's internal response, and what was God's reaction? What does this teach us about faith?

....

....

....

....

....

So far, Abram has been promised:

> God will make of you a great nation.
> God will give you a baby this year.
> God will give you a son as an heir.
> God will give you a baby through Sarai.

What mood or emotion might Abram have come home with after this experience with God?

....

....

....

God wanted Abram to "know for certain" (Genesis 15:13) that he would keep his promises, so he called this former moon-worshiper out of his tent to gaze up at a canopy of stars. *This is what your family photo will look like. You won't even be able to count them all.* Then Abram "believed the LORD, and counted it to him as righteousness" (Genesis 15:6).

Genesis 15 was a mountaintop experience for Abram, but in Genesis 16, Abram's wife is in the valley. As far as we know, Sarai didn't get to see the smoking firepot or go stargazing with God. So when enthusiastic, faith-filled Abram starts recounting God's promises, I picture Sarai not dancing for joy, but swallowing the lump in her throat and brushing aside tears.

Yes, she knew about God's grandiose promises. But she also knew she was still living in a tent. And still childless.

A Locked Door

Sarai must have been elated when she first learned God had promised Abram would become father not just to a child, but to a nation! And she must have become slowly confused, then devastated, when month after month God left the parenthesis of his promise open.

promise made

If you or I found the door to motherhood locked, we would have specialists to see, agencies to consider, or other doors to knock on. For Sarai, motherhood was the only door, and there was no one to unlock it. Not only was Sarai's dignity inextricably tied to having a baby, God's promises hinged on her ability to conceive.

Imagine the pressure and defeat of having to respond month after month when Abram discreetly asked, "So . . . any news?" Sarai not only couldn't produce a baby, she had a husband who believed she could.

Write out Genesis 11:30.

....

....

....

Write out the first half of Genesis 16:1.

....

....

....

Check your timeline on page 17. How old is Sarai, and how many years has she likely struggled with infertility?

....

How many monthly disappointments has Sarai endured (use your math) in the promised land?

....

How do you suppose she felt about God's promises after Abram's mountaintop, stargazing experience?

....

....

....

....

Sarai's Brittle Branch

From the beginning, our Bible uses trees to image people. Even in the creation poem (Genesis 1), on days three and six, there is a parallel drawn between fruit trees and people—both of which bear "fruit with seed in it" (Genesis 1:12).[1] God designed us to be fruitful! One of the main themes of Genesis is watching "seed" (often translated "offspring") pass from one generation to the next, as family trees explode with fruitfulness.

After Adam and Eve ate the forbidden fruit, God gives his most precious promise: the seed (offspring) of the woman will crush the snake (Genesis 3:15). Our promised Savior—the one who will free us by eradicating evil—won't come in the clouds. (At least not the first time.) He'll be born. He'll be part of someone's family tree. So from this point on, as we turn the pages of Genesis and meet each new generation, we're asking, "Is it time? Has the promised offspring been born?" Then God singles out Abram, promising that all the families of the world will be blessed through him (Genesis 12:3), and we start connecting the dots. At last! But our excitement is cut short when we learn something devastating: Abram's wife Sarai is barren. She's a brittle branch on the family tree, not a fruitful one.

Notice what God is saying as he selects a brittle branch to produce his promised offspring. Whether on fruit trees or family trees, God makes the fruit grow. He is the Creator. Fruitfulness of any form is a gift from him. Yet God knows how we gravitate to self-reliance, so with his promised offspring, he is making double sure we understand: self-salvation is not possible. Sarai is barren and cannot produce what God has promised. Yet we're about to see her try.

Read Genesis 16:1–3.

What did Sarai say was the cause of her infertility? Is she correct?

....

....

....

....

Is Sarai being shaped by God's promises? What indicators do you see in the text?

....

....

....

How does her response contrast with Abram's in Genesis 15:5–6?

....

....

....

Gaby's Narrowing Possibilities

We've all felt the stabbing pain of dashed hopes as we navigate this world, sagging under the brokenness of sin and the fall. Women, in particular, experience the heartsick sorrow of infertility, marriage, and longing for a family. My friend Gaby knows this pain well.

Gaby has always longed to be a mother. She figured by age twenty-seven, God would at least have given her a husband. Instead, God has given her stage-three breast cancer. Once Gaby finishes treatment, she'll begin a ten-year medication that causes infertility and early menopause. For Gaby, the possibility of having children is narrowing.

"Why, God?" she's asked, in despair. But Gaby also sees her years of chewing on fork-and-knife theology in her biblical counseling training as God's preparation for this painful path between her trials and the promises of eternity to come. It's not a path to be rushed, Gaby says. It's a time to know and savor God in his Word. It's a time to let him prune and grow his fruit.

Gaby recently went through her journals, looking for other instances of God's faithfulness in the past—knowing he was the same then as on these dark days. Her eyes widened when she came across an entry where she had written, "God, I want to know and understand you more! I want to experience you in my life. I'm so tired of my sin." God was using cancer to answer her prayer, for she has found God to be sweeter and more present in her suffering than ever before. And while she prays the treatment will heal her of cancer, she recognizes it's also healing her of her sin—in particular her self-reliance and her desire for control.

Gaby knows she has no promise of becoming a mother, or even regaining her health. So what promise does Gaby cling to? She clings to God, who is better than sons and daughters (Isaiah 56:5), and who promises her eternal life with him.

When I listen to Gaby talk, I see her life blossoming with spiritual fruit as she is shaped by God's promises. Has God forgotten or abandoned Gaby? Absolutely not. He is tending to her soul daily (2 Corinthians 4:16), faithful as ever. In the middle of Gaby's cancer, God is keeping his promise to never leave (Hebrews 13:5), and to give comfort (2 Corinthians 1:4) and peace (Philippians 4:7). He is reminding Gaby that nothing can separate her from his love (Romans 8:39). God is giving Gaby himself!

Though Sarai couldn't see it, God was faithful as ever to her as well, even in the middle of her infertility. He had not forgotten or abandoned Sarai. Her future was no less sure. In that wide stretch between the parentheses, God was

Listen to more of Gaby Puente's story on Shannon's Live Like It's True podcast. Go to shannonpopkin.com /promises.

demonstrating what a collapsed timeline couldn't: he is faithful, and he alone produces fruit.

Your Brittle Branch

What are you in the middle of today? How are you desperate for fruitfulness? Perhaps you, too, long for the honor of being a mom or grandma. Maybe you ache to see your work or investment bear fruit. Or perhaps there's some spiritual fruit you are desperate for. Do you yearn to break free from an addiction, pornography, or an affair? Do you long to be patient, not angry? To have peace, not anxiety?

Or perhaps it's the spiritual fruit on someone else's branches that you yearn to see. Has your marriage been bruised by unfaithfulness and deceit? Has your adult child walked away from his faith? Do you long for your brother to return to his wife, or your daughter to return your calls? Is your dad addicted to alcohol, or your teen to pornography?

Sister, could it be that in this wide stretch, God wants you to remember that he alone produces fruitfulness?

What brittle branch are you agonizing over? What fruit do you long for?

....

....

....

....

Describe how you feel about the fruit you haven't been able to produce.

....

....

....

....

How has God used this situation to help you recognize that he alone is in control?

....

....

....

Read Psalm 1:1–3. How can you be like the tree described here?

....

....

....

....

....

When God Prevents

If infertility is part of your story, oh how God grieves with you. This painful effect of the fall is never what God intended when he created a world exploding with fruitfulness. Because God loves you, he promises to one day peel back sin's corruption from the whole earth so you can experience life as you were meant to in that Garden City of heaven. In order for this to happen, God sent his promised offspring to crush sin's power and eradicate evil.

This is the plan God is setting in motion when he promises Sarai's brittle branch will bear fruit. But then years go by with no fruit. God *prevents* the fruit (Genesis 16:2), and Sarai can't figure out why. Can you? Do you see the reason for God lingering so, before dropping that second parenthesis of his promises?

Remember, back in the introduction, those two things that God can only accomplish between widened parentheses? Check back on pages 13–15 if you need a refresher, and fill in the blanks. Then consider God's fruit-producing work in Sarai's life, and your own.

1. God's _____ is _____ over time.

2. God wants us to be _____ by his _____.

promise made

(⟵————————————————————⟶

If Sarai had immediately become pregnant, how might she have missed out on one or both of these?

....

....

....

How has God, the masterful storyteller, held Sarai's attention and ours so far in the story?

....

....

....

Consider your own "brittle branch":

How has God held your attention by not skipping too quickly to the "good part"?

....

....

....

....

What have you discovered about God's faithfulness in the waiting?

....

....

....

....

....

....

The Sequel Coming

My friend Abigail overheard her daughter, Eliza, say she had finished her book. Then, Eliza's brother asked, "Was it a happy ending or a sad ending?"

"It was a happy ending," Eliza said, and he was glad. But then Eliza said, "Oh, but I like the sad endings best, because it means there's a sequel coming."[2]

Sister, it was true for Sarai, and it's true of you. There's a sequel coming! God can cause any dead thing in your life to burst into bloom at any moment. So in that sense, perhaps he has prevented something you long for. But there is a day coming when God will wipe every tear from your eyes and make all things new (Revelation 21:4–5). God will keep his promises—every one of them!

Oh, how we want to skip to the good part—yet this stretch between the parentheses *is* one of the good parts. Will you allow your desperation for fruitfulness to lift your eyes to the One who produces fruit? Will you choose to be shaped by his promises? The wait is never wasted. God's faithfulness can only be known over time.

Stapling Up Fruit

In Sarai's culture, people got married to have children. A love story wasn't necessary but children were. Since Sarai was a wife with no child and Abram was the clan "father" who had no son, their marriage was seen as a failure.[3] They were like a school with no students or a store with no shoppers. Their childlessness brought them not just sorrow but shame. Yet through their story, God shows us that self-reliance isn't the answer.

Read Genesis 16:1–4.

When God introduced himself to Abram, his first words were, "I will, I will, I will." Now ten years later, Sarai's first recorded words are, "Perhaps I can . . ." After a decade of waiting for God to keep his promises, Sarai is taking matters into her own hands.

How is Sarai trying to take control? How are control and faith at odds with each other?

....

....

....

....

....

....

What can Hagar not control? What implies that she sees herself gaining control?

....

....

....

Is Hagar's pregnancy the result of God keeping his promises? How would Sarai answer that question?

....

....

....

....

Look at the New International Version translation of verse 2:

> **Go, sleep with my slave; perhaps I can _____ a family through her.**

This is one of those Hebrew words made from concrete imagery, not abstraction. Sarai sees this baby as a building block to prop her whole life on. After a decade of waiting on God, I imagine Sarai thinking, *We left our home, our family, our life. We've been living in a foreign country for ten years. We've done everything God asked! Why hasn't he blessed us with a child?*

Have you ever felt that way? Perhaps you saved sex for marriage, you've lived by your convictions at work, or you raised your kids to love God—and you wonder why, oh why, hasn't God blessed you like you imagined he would? Sister, God *is* pleased with your obedience, but he's not interested in a transactional relationship with you. He invites you to live like it's true that he is God and you are not—by surrendering control to him. Sarai misunderstands and does the opposite.

Trying to Play God

Look back at Genesis 16:1-3 and list out what Sarai can and cannot control:

CAN CONTROL	CANNOT CONTROL

How is Sarai trying to take over and play God?

....

....

....

"Nobody who tries to play God does a very good job of it." Is this a true statement? Why or why not?

....

....

....

You might wonder if we're being unfairly critical to accuse Sarai of "playing God" when she offers Hagar to Abram. After all, God has not yet explicitly stated that Sarai will be the mother of Abram's promised child. Nor does God directly reprimand the Abrams for having a child this way.[4] To be clear, I am interpreting—not observing—the text when I say that "The Hagar Solution" is a plan void of faith. Here's what leads me to this interpretation.

Moses isn't simply chronicling the events of Abram and Sarai's life. He's crafting this episode from Genesis 16 as part of a larger framework. He's telling the Wildernites' origin story, remember? It's a story that is all about God making and keeping promises to his chosen people. One of the story's main tensions—the thing that jeopardizes many of the promises—is Sarai's barrenness (Genesis 11:30). By the end of the story,[5] we (the readers) will see what the Wildernites already know: the child born to Abram through Hagar is not only irrelevant to their origin story, he's a threat.

In addition, the New Testament uses Sarai's "Hagar Solution" as an example of self-reliance (see Galatians 4:22–23), which is the opposite of walking by faith. God is teaching Sarai (and all of us who know her story) that self-reliance jeopardizes our faith.

Exchanging Shame for Honor

Sarai hoped she could reverse the shame of her infertility and recover her honor by stapling her own fruit onto the family tree. Now, through our own cultural lens, this is hard to understand. We look at Sarai's "Hagar solution" and wonder, *Who in the world would give her husband another woman to sleep with?* We imagine this adding to Sarai's shame, not recovering her honor. But in Sarai's culture, surrogacy was not only legal, it was expected. In fact, marriage contracts from this era have been discovered that include infertility clauses giving the husband the right to a concubine if after two years his wife has not given birth.[6]

Sarai had been a childless wife for a lot longer than two years, so perhaps she thought of her plan as honorable. It's possible that she even thought that God would be pleased. He was the one who had promised Abram his descendants would be as numerous as the stars (Genesis 15:5). She was the one providing the surrogate to make it happen.

For Sarai, this could undo the shame of her childlessness, since any baby born to Hagar would legally count as fruit on Sarai's branch of the family tree. If you (like me) find this horrifying and want to reach into the story and protect vulnerable Hagar, don't worry. God is going to do that very thing at the end of Genesis 16. But before you wrinkle your nose at the sin smeared across this page of your Bible, let me warn you of a danger.

If you and I look down at Sarai and her culture in condescending disgust, we might miss seeing ourselves in her story. Sarai's culture saw no need to consult God on its baby-procurement strategies of polygamy, forced surrogacy, or slavery. In a similar way, many cultures today see no need to consult God on their baby-*reduction* strategy of abortion. Sarai was simply caving to the demands of her particular culture; she's trying to play God and produce a baby of her own making. But consider the irony: God doesn't cave to the demands of anyone. He is both free enough and powerful enough to do whatever he pleases.

Think of how we—like Sarai—tend to hyperfocus on our own little world, indifferent to everyone else, when we lunge for control. We play God, convinced that we not only can take control, we *should* take control. But in doing so, we reveal how very unlike God we really are. God manages the whole world with love. He is good, kind, and self-sacrificing. (Just think of the cross.) His goodness spills over into the lives of those we overlook, and his purposes span out to people on the timeline we haven't even imagined. He invites us to entrust ourselves to his good, all-powerful hands, instead of our scrawny, controlling ones.

Name at least one present-day example of:

People succumbing to demands of culture

....

....

People trying to control each other

....

....

People seeing no need to consult God

....

....

People playing God by restructuring marriage, family, and children

....

....

Think of the pressures you feel from your culture. Think also of sub-cultures, such as your family, church, or friend group. How have you wrongly caved in to demands?

....

....

....

How have you tried to play God by controlling others? Who have you been selfishly indifferent toward?

....

....

....

The Bigger Story

So often our control efforts stem from our small-storied perspective. As Sarai tries to staple her own fruit onto her family tree, she is focused only on her own little story. Our Bibles tell a story which inextricably involves Sarai, yet is all about God. Take a step back and consider.

God promised not just a baby for one couple, but a Savior for the world. God looks down the timeline to the cross, where this promised offspring will give his life and deal with humanity's greatest problem: sin and death. Do you see the magnitude of what God has promised for Sarai's family tree? And do you see how scrawny Sarai's hands look as she reaches for her stapler?

If God wrote the story of our salvation as a transactional arrangement—our work exchanged for forgiveness and eternal life—we'd surely become self-reliant like Sarai and self-exalting like Hagar. We would focus on what we can and should do, not what God has done. But God knew our propensity toward self-salvation and self-exaltation, which is why he *alone* walked the aisle through the pieces.

God makes the promises. God keeps the promises. And God invites us to believe his promises will come true, then live accordingly.

How is God's way of salvation the opposite of transactional? How have you twisted it into a transactional arrangement?

....

....

....

What pride, perfectionism, or other self-salvation tendencies do you see in yourself?

....

....

....

For the Christian, why are self-reliance and pride both inappropriate responses?

....

....

....

....

....

Stapling Up Fruit

Centuries later, Paul wrote a letter to the Galatians—a church made up of non-Jews, who nevertheless were "children of Abraham" because they had Abraham's faith (Galatians 3:7). Abraham and Sarah had looked forward with faith to the promised offspring (Jesus); the Galatians looked back with faith to Jesus. Throughout his letter, Paul speaks of salvation as a transfer called "justification," in which Jesus became the "sinner" so sinners could become the "righteous."[7] And what is required for this transfer to take place? We simply believe God's promise that this will save us, and we are justified—for good.

The Galatians believed this at first, but then Jews (descendants of Abraham) showed up, saying, "But what about all of our laws? *True* children of Abraham do better and try harder." So the Galatians assumed that in order to *stay* forgiven and *become* righteous, they would have to adopt this "do better, try harder" mindset. But Paul adamantly refuted this and argued his case by pointing to the self-reliance of Sarah and Abraham.

Read Galatians 4:22–23.

Hagar's son was born as a result of:

....

....

Hagar's son was not born (as Sarah's will be) through:

....

....

What do Abraham's true children have, according to Galatians 3:7?

....

....

What about those who rely on the law? See Galatians 3:10.

....

....

....

How are we justified? See Galatians 3:11.

....

....

....

....

....

Faith begins where self-reliance ends. And faith ends where self-reliance begins. Paul was pointing to this reality in Sarah's story, showing that when she turned to Hagar, she turned *from* faith. She chose human effort over God's promises. Therefore, Hagar's child was irrelevant to God's promises.

All along, God knew having a baby wasn't something Sarah could do; he planned it that way. He wanted the Galatians, us, and everyone in between to know that salvation is not our work, but his. And it's the same with the spiritual fruit that comes *after* our salvation. This is the work of his Spirit in us, not the fruit of self-effort.

How have you tried to "staple up fruit" and project a façade of spiritual fruitfulness? What is your motivation for doing so?

....

....

....

How is self-reliant, stapled-up fruit different from true, spiritual fruit?

....

....

....

Why is fruit-stapling often a response to shame and inadequacy?

....

....

....

....

Stapling Fruit over Shame

Back when my boys were in elementary school, they used our basement storage room to spread out their LEGOs and build elaborate towers. I asked them to go clean it up one day because guests were coming over. An hour later, I went down and surveyed the remaining mess, and—in a horrible fit of rage, I did something awful. I smashed the tower they had been working on for months.

Immediately, my heart filled with sickening regret. What had I done? As the boys came running into the room, their looks of shock and horror are still frozen in my memory. "Oh, noooo!" they said, seeing all of their work shattered on the floor. "Boys, I'm so sorry," I said. "I don't know why I did that . . . Mommy is so, so sorry!"

My husband, hearing the commotion, came in as well and immediately said, "Kids, get in the car." Obediently, they filed out of the room, then he turned to me, and said, "Shannon, your anger is tearing this family down! I need you to think about what you're doing here."

I fell to a heap of guilt and shame. *What was wrong with me? What kind of mother would do such a thing?* And now, what could I do? There was no way to undo the damage. I was alone with my shame, regret, and sorrow. And do you know what my first inclination was, there on the basement floor? It was not to ask God for help. It was to wield the shame into a fruit-stapling resolve. *Shannon, you are ridiculous. You've got to turn this around. From now on, you're going to be the kindest, most patient mom ever to live. You've got to make up for this.*

Do you see the progression? When confronted with the shame of my sin, I turned to self-reliance and control. And yet I had just demonstrated how ugly things get when I'm the one trying to control it all. Without God's help, I can't even produce *self*-control!

It's true that my behavior was shameful and wrong, but fruit-stapling isn't the solution. *Jesus* is my solution. Only God could save me from sin, and only God can grow fruit on the spiritually brittle branches of my life. I can't grit my teeth and grow this fruit on my own. Jesus said, "I am the vine; you are the branches. . . . Apart from me you can do nothing" (John 15:5). Growing spiritual fruit is not a try-harder, do-better process. It's a process of surrendering control to God—for even self-control is a fruit of the Spirit (Galatians 5:23).

When Sarai does finally conceive, God will make it infinitely clear that her baby is a result of his power, not hers. It's the same with our spiritual fruit. Any fruit that grows on our brittle branches is evidence of God's Spirit and his power—not us getting a white-knuckled grip on our staplers.

Look through the list of "works of the flesh" in Galatians 5:19–21. Which are true of you? Ask God to bring several examples to mind:

....

....

....

Look through the fruit of the Spirit listed in Galatians 5:22–23. Which are true of you? Ask God to bring several examples to mind:

....

....

....

What does the Spirit want you to remember about yourself in Galatians 4:6?

....

....

....

In self-reliance, we might be able to staple up some self-made fruit, which looks good from a distance. But those who know us best know our stapled-on fruit isn't genuine and won't last. The real fruit is produced over time as we rely on his Spirit to change us from the inside out.

Picture a dead-looking fruit tree gradually coming to life. First there are tiny buds of green, then blossoms and small leaves. After a nourishing season, bright-colored fruit spots the branches. Over the years, the roots sink deeper, and the tree expands. Its trunk thickens, and its twigs become sturdy branches, loaded with fruit. This is what it looks like to be shaped by God's promises.

Passive Husband, Controlling Wife

On a wooded trail in Costa Rica, Ken and I came across a black widow spider that must have been two inches long. The spider froze, and we did, too—except for my tongue. "Don't move! I think we're supposed to stay still. Or run? Are we supposed to run? Maybe we should throw something . . ."

I shudder to think of how easily I could have pushed for a very hasty, bad idea. I read later[8] that you should never rush at, throw something at, or try to squish a black widow (all ideas that had crossed my mind) because it will probably charge at you. Horrors! Thankfully, the spider apparently got bored with my high-pitched verbal processing and scurried off into the woods.

It was interesting to me that as we faced a dangerous threat, I talked and Ken didn't. These were both our intuitive responses. This was a pattern for Abram and Sarai as well, though not over something morally ambiguous (like whether to squish a big spider). No, the idea Sarai was talking about and pushing for was one which denied the promises God had given. It was a bad idea, void of faith.

Read Genesis 16:1–6.

Who does most of the talking? Is his or her tone passive or aggressive?

....

....

Who does very little talking? Is his or her tone passive or aggressive?

....

....

Abram and Hagar

Sarai most likely met Hagar in Egypt, when she was taken into Pharaoh's harem. Was Hagar assigned to Sarai? Did she draw Sarai's bath and comb her hair? We don't know for sure, but most commentators suppose that when Genesis 12:16 says, "[Pharaoh] treated Abram well because of [Sarai], and Abram acquired flocks and herds . . . male and female slaves" (CSB), one of those slaves who left Egypt with Abram and Sarai was Hagar.

Now remember, the Bible is descriptive, not prescriptive when it says that our walk-by-faith pioneers owned slaves. God does not condone slavery! Nor does he condone what happens next.

Here's my three-word summary of Genesis 16:3:

Abram married Hagar.

Count how many words your Bible takes in Genesis 16:3 to say the same thing:

....

What descriptors are added for each person in Genesis 16:3 and why?

....

....

....

....

....

Our Bibles use all of those extra words to loudly proclaim that our relationships—especially marriage—are precious to God. Moses (the author of Genesis) expressed God's high view of marriage back in Genesis 2 when he described marriage as a husband and wife becoming one flesh (Genesis 2:24). Yet here in this scene we have a wife suggesting her husband marry an additional woman—and that woman had no choice.

Again, the Bible here is descriptive, not prescriptive. It's likely that Abram and Sarai were so influenced by culture, they had no idea that adding Hagar to their marriage was even the slightest bit wrong. Still, our storyteller Moses signals his disapproval by drawing a parallel between this scene and the one in Genesis 3 which got the first couple kicked out of Eden.[9] From his perspective, the worst of history was repeating itself.

Sarai and Eve

Record the particular action verb used to link Sarai's story with Eve's:

Genesis 16:2 says, "And Abram _____ to the voice of Sarai."

In Genesis 3:17, God says to Adam, "Because you _____ to the voice of your wife..."

Ordinarily, we think of attentiveness in marriage as good, right? But in these two instances, the husband was listening to his wife *instead* of rehearsing what God had said. He was lending an ear, not leading. Scholar Derek Kidner writes, "[Abram] had slipped from faith, to be guided by reason and the voice of Sarai, not of the Lord."[10]

Read and compare these two stories:

	ADAM & EVE	ABRAM & SARAI
What important information did God give the husband (not the wife)?	Genesis 2:5-17	Genesis 15:3-4
What did the wife "take" and "give"?	Genesis 3:6	Genesis 16:3
What did the wife do to influence her husband? (It's inferred.)	Genesis 3:17	Genesis 16:2
What was the husband influenced by his wife to do?	Genesis 3:6	Genesis 16:4

In both instances, the husband was listening, which means the wife was talking. Both times, there was a high-stake, spider-in-the-path sort of decision to be made and the wife influenced her husband to respond with self-reliance, not faith. Both times, rather than speaking up about the direct-from-God information entrusted to him, the husband stayed silent. Rather than stewarding God's words that his wife desperately needed to be reminded of, he passively let her take control and received the forbidden fruit she placed in his hands.

This "controlling wife/passive husband" pattern is not only true of Bible couples.

Describe the effect it has on a marriage when the wife takes control.

....

....

....

Describe the effect it has on a marriage when the husband is typically passive.

....

....

....

The Head and the Neck

There's a scene in the movie, *My Big Fat Greek Wedding*, where Toula is crying because she doesn't think her dad will allow her to marry her non-Greek boyfriend. Her mother tries to console her, saying she'll talk to him. But Toula, convinced he won't budge, mimics her father, saying, "Da man is da head of da house."

"Let me tell you something, Toula," her mother says. "The man is the head, but the woman is the neck, and she can turn the head any way she wants."[11] I think we all laugh at that scene because we know there's some truth to it. As a wife, I have ways of being "the neck." I know how to manipulate, talk over, emasculate, and demean my husband to get my way. I know that most often, when I grab the reigns, my husband will not fight me for them. It's the same pattern we've just seen in Eve and Sarai's stories.

So why shouldn't a wife just go ahead and be the neck—or even the head—in her marriage? Why shouldn't she step in and take control?[12] The idea that husbands are to lead is certainly not a popular idea, but I want you to see where it comes from.

Paul, the author of Ephesians, cites the very first marriage in Genesis 2–3 as the basis for his candid instruction on this subject (Ephesians 5:31). Let's look at both passages:

	ADAM AND EVE
Who was formed first? How was the second one formed? Genesis 2:7, 22	
Who was directly given the warning, and what does this imply? Genesis 2:15–18	
Who did God call to account first, and what does this imply? Genesis 3:9	
Who named whom, and what does this imply? Genesis 3:20	
Are you convinced that God chose Adam to be the leader? Why or why not?	

What instructions are given... Ephesians 5:22-32	to husbands?	to wives?

Are you convinced that God chose husbands to be leaders? Why or why not?

The Metaphor and Mystery of Marriage

If I throw my wedding ring down and let it bounce across the floor like a worthless trinket, I disrespect not only the ring, which has value in its own right, but also my marriage, which the ring symbolizes. Similarly, if I am careless or hostile toward my marriage, I disrespect not only the marriage, which has value in its own right, but also the relationship which the marriage points to.

Marriage has always been about more than marriage. It points to something more. Paul, the writer of Ephesians, unveils the mystery (Ephesians 5:23) by explaining that marriage is meant to illustrate God's love for us. One reason God created brides and grooms and marriage was so he could point and say, "See that? Jesus loves you like a groom loves his bride."

When we get married, Paul says we participate in reenacting the gospel story of Christ and his church. But do you see the potential we have to mar and distort the gospel? When a wife manipulates, undermines, or berates her husband, or when a husband abuses his wife or passively shrugs at her sin, we disrespect marriage and distort the bigger story it points to. So in Ephesians 5, Paul shows us how to realign our marriages with God's beautiful gospel story. Husbands reenact the story by sacrificially loving their wives. Wives reenact the story by submitting to their husbands (Ephesians 5:25, 22).

Describe the sweetest wedding you've witnessed (or watched in a movie). How does this help you understand Christ's love for you?

....

....

....

Read Ephesians 5:22–32.

Look for the words "that" or "to" to find the reason Christ gave himself up for his bride:

....

....

....

What washes the bride (v. 26)?

....

....

....

....

Soaking in the Promises

God's word is like a tub full of fresh water. Recalling what God has said is like taking a bath in his promises. To soak in God's word is to cleanse our motives and purify our ideations. And according to Ephesians, the husband's responsibility is to "draw the bath," so to speak. He is to remind his wife of God's instruction and promises, which refresh her faith.

What if Adam had courageously stepped between his wife and the serpent? What if Abram had courageously stepped between Sarai and Hagar? What if these husbands had renounced passivity and spoken up? They had been entrusted with God's words, which had huge implications for their families.

Now, neither husband had been entrusted with all the answers. In Abram's case, God hasn't yet explicitly stated that he would have a son with Sarai. (He will in Genesis 17:21.) But as we watch the Abrams' story unfold, we are learning what it means to walk by faith, not sight. God often asks his people to move forward without all of the information—not in self-reliance, but in dependence on God, rehearsing what he *has* said and promised.

When a husband courageously leads his wife to God's word and promises, he helps her wash away her pride and self-sufficiency and invites her to faith. Husbands are to lead in this way, and wives are to let them—or maybe even invite them.

Stop Talking

I've taught enough on this subject to know that the minute I say husbands are to lead, there will be a wife saying, *"But he won't lead!"* or *"He doesn't want to!"* And I get it. My marriage naturally defaults to the "passive husband/controlling wife" pattern.

I not only *want* to take control, I convince myself I *should*. I feel justified yanking the reigns out of my husband's hands—especially when somebody's wrong, somebody's going to get hurt, or somebody isn't taking responsibility. It's times like these when—like Eve and Sarai before me—I want Ken to "listen to the voice of Shannon." I want him to do what *I* say. But I only introduce tension and strife.

I think my sisters who don't believe in marital role distinctions will conclude the same. When a wife tries to talk over or talk down to her husband, insisting that he does what she wants, has she not just broken the equality? There are moments when it feels so *right* to use loud, belligerent words to get my husband to listen to me. Yet, in order to lead well, my husband needs to hear from God, not me. Which means that I need to stop talking.

Let me give you a recent example to illustrate.

Inviting Him to Lead

Ken and I were driving to meet one of our adult kids for lunch when I asked, "Are you planning to ask those questions Daryll suggested?"

He said, "Shannon, you're always so pushy. Do we need an agenda? Let's just have lunch with our son."

He was right; I do often have an agenda. My big hopes for our kids are often accompanied by big concerns. I extrapolate, fret, and heap the burden of control back on my shoulders, convinced that I must make everything turn out right. My husband often reminds me to trust God, not myself. But, still. Daryll's questions were helpful, and it wasn't wrong for me to suggest them—and actually by doing so ahead of time, I was inviting Ken to lead. So in response to his reminder that I don't need to impose my agenda on every conversation, I said, "I'll receive that. And I will support you either way. I just wanted to remind you of Daryll's questions because I thought they were good."

He said, "What were those questions again?"

Ken did end up using the questions, which resulted in a fruitful conversation. And see how my choice made that possible? I told him I'd *be supportive either way*. I offered my honest thoughts and then invited him to lead.

Now, I have done it the other way, more times than I can count. I've been a pushy, demeaning, argumentative wife, grabbing for control with white-knuckled demands. And like in Sarai's story and Eve's, this has brought such heartache. But when I pattern my marriage after God's design, I invite freedom and wholeness.

What if Eve had said, "Adam, I'll support whatever you say. Should we eat this fruit?" What if Sarai had said, "Abram, I'll support whatever you say. Is Hagar the solution?" What if you or I said to our husbands, "I'll support whatever you say. Should we . . . ?" When a wife invites her husband to lead, she invites him to consider God's voice and not just her own.

As a wife, what situations have you been trying to control? How have you been more invested in getting your husband to listen to you than listen to God?

....

....

....

....

How will you invite your husband to lead? How will you show your support when he does lead?

....

....

....

....

....

How will you support husbands leading in the other marriages where you have influence?

....

....

....

....

....

What two direction-setting items does James compare the tongue to in James 3:3–5? In what relationship or setting is God asking you to stop talking so others can be steered by God (not you)?

....

....

....

....

....

....

....

....

....

....

Pointing Fingers, Naming Names

It had to have been awkward. Did Sarai move out of Abram's tent completely? Did she let Hagar borrow a nightgown? Was Hagar repulsed at the thought of sharing her eighty-five-year-old master's bed?

Whatever the details, Hagar became pregnant. And that's when the relational foundation beneath this unborn babe began to quake. Sarai had been so desperate for the honor she believed this baby would achieve for her. But when Hagar misses her period, everything seesaws in a direction Sarai wasn't expecting.

Read Genesis 16:4–5.

What body language might Hagar have used to communicate what is stated in verse 4?

....

....

How did Hagar begin to see Sarai differently? How does this imply Hagar sees *herself* differently?

....

....

Consider both women's reactions. What can you conclude about their view of motherhood and this pregnancy?

....

....

Who does Sarai go to (v. 5)? What tone and demeanor do her words imply?

....

....

Compare what the narrator reports about Hagar with what Sarai reports (vv. 4–5).

    Is Sarai's report accurate?

....

....

    Is her assessment of who's to blame accurate? Why or why not?

....

....

....

Which two people is Sarai calling God to judge between (v. 5)?

....

What relevance does Proverbs 30:21-23 have?

....

....

....

When Genesis 16:4 says that Hagar looked at Sarai with contempt, the text literally reads, "her mistress looked little to her."[13] Do you see what's happening? It seems that Hagar, too, recognizes this pregnancy as a huge building block, only she sees *herself* as the one elevated. She's the one carrying Abram's child. She has accomplished what Sarai couldn't. From way up on her pregnancy pedestal, Sarai looks unimportant and small.

The Costliness of Control

I have so much compassion for Sarai as she deals with the disgrace of this situation unraveling before her eyes. She saw Hagar as the solution; she thought this baby would provide a building block out of her pit of shame. But stepping on others (even if it's culturally acceptable) to lift yourself up is never the answer. Jesus taught, "Everyone who exalts [herself] will be humbled" (Luke 14:11), and that's what I see happening.

When Sarai tries to play God and move people like chess pieces into the beds that suited her purposes, she didn't count the cost.

Your Bible probably translates Sarai saying something like, "I gave my servant to your embrace" (Genesis 16:5), but the Hebrew euphemism she used was crasser than that. It's a sexual innuendo that translates, "I put my servant in your lap."[14] Do you hear the deep hurt, embarrassment, and humiliation spewing out with Sarai's words? Consider the cauldron of emotions she's dealing with:

WHAT HAPPENED	HOW SARAI LIKELY FELT ABOUT IT
Sarai gave Hagar to Abram as a wife.	
Hagar is obviously fertile.	
Abram now has the child he has longed for.	
Abram's line will continue without Sarai's help.	

Abram isn't the infertile one. It's confirmed.	
Hagar is looking at Sarai with contempt.	
Sarai's plan to gain honor is backfiring.	

All of this comes at great cost to Sarai. She has gone from public humiliation to personal disgrace. And is Abram over there *enjoying* this new arrangement at her expense? Hagar sure seems to be!

As Sarai speaks of the "wrong" done to her (Genesis 16:5), the word she uses is one for violence. Kent Hughes says, "Her soul felt as though she were the victim of a homicide."[15] And who died? Sarai the Great. Sarai the Mother. Sarai the Hopeful.

Sarai feels like all of God's promise parentheses are closing, and she's left on the outside, mourning what will never be. This isn't true, of course. Our emotions can't be trusted to tell the full story.

What if Sarai had returned to God's word? What if she had soaked in the promises to help level out her emotions? Instead, Sarai did what we often do when control slips from our grasp: she brought her hot anger to someone she had influence over, demanding answers.

Trial by Sarai

Genesis 16:5—when Sarai barges in on Abram—reads like a court case. Look carefully at Sarai's words and the implications she is making. According to Sarai, who is

The victim? ....

The one responsible for the victim's suffering? ....

The perpetrator? ....

The offender or criminal? ....

The supreme judge? ....

The innocent party? ....

The guilty and liable party? ....

Who do *you* see as the greatest victim?

....

....

....

Since Abram is the decision maker, he plays the role of "district judge," but he seems to lack the wisdom and compassion required for the job. I picture him in a recliner, barely even looking up from his reading material, as Sarai charges in to make her case.

What is Abram's "ruling" in Genesis 16:6?

....

....

....

What does Sarai do afterward?

....

....

....

Compare Abram's responses to Sarai in Genesis 16:2 and 16:6. Choose the correct word.

> In 16:6, Abram is more | equally | less passive.

Compare Sarah's actions in Genesis 16:2 and 16:6. Choose the correct word.

> In 16:6, Sarai is more | equally | less controlling.

Character Evaluation

In a good story, we see characters develop and grow, but in this one Abram and Sarai are stagnantly stuck in their pattern of "controlling wife/passive husband." As Sarai loses her grip on control, she frantically tries to regain her dignity by pointing her finger and picking up God's gavel.

She's the victim. Look at all she's lost! This makes Abram the guilty party, right? And yet, Sarai fails to consider a third possibility: What if she and Abram are both wrong?

Evaluate each of the characters in our story, using the character traits from Galatians 5:19–26.

	NOBLE, right character qualities	HARMFUL, wrong character qualities
Abram		
Sarai		
Hagar		

Did you have some gaping holes in that first column? Sister, this story has no hero. As Sarai bangs her gavel, she only reveals her blindness to how wrong *she* has been.

No one in this story is being shaped by God's promises. No one is soaking in the goodness of God's faithfulness. Everyone is acting like there *are* no promises, and there *is* no God who says, "I will." And everyone is paying the price.

Read James 4:1–3. What is the cause of Sarai and Abram's conflict, according to this passage?

....

....

....

Based on these verses, what advice would you give to Sarai at this point?

....

....

....

What conflict are you experiencing? How might your advice for Sarai be applicable to you?

....

....

....

....

The Progression of Control

When Sarai comes to Abram with her crass language and pointing finger, she wants security and assurance. She needs her leader to lead and protect her. Ultimately she wants control of an out-of-control situation.

But do you see the pattern? As Sarai lunges with white knuckles at her husband, he reverts to the least satisfying response of all: passivity.

"Do whatever you want," Abram says (Genesis 16:6 csb). He's deferring to another cultural law which says a concubine who claims equality with her mistress after pregnancy can be demoted to her former (slave) status.[16] Abram's passivity only diverts Sarai's fury in a new direction. Poor Hagar had no defense against Sarai's wounded, frustrated rage.

Look carefully at the progression of control and where it leads. First Sarai tried to take control by stapling her own fruit on her family tree. But she lost control when she was humiliated by Hagar rather than being lifted up. Next she tried to control her husband by guilting him into leading responsibly. But he abdicated his influence and Sarai lost control of the one thing that was hers to control: herself.

There were lots of things here that Sarai couldn't control, but could she have controlled her words? Her rage? Her mind? Her heart? For ten years, she's been living as a stranger in a tent, waiting for God to close the parenthesis (Hebrews 11:13–16). What if she had chosen to wait ten more? What needless suffering could she have avoided and prevented? It's a valuable question for us to ask ourselves as well.

Hold and Fold

Surrender to God involves a "hold and fold" approach. First, we hold responsibility for ourselves, stewarding the influence we have over others. With everything else, we fold our hands in surrender to God.

What have you been trying to control that you cannot?

....

....

....

....

Check your heart for any of the following, which are rooted in a desire for control. Ask for God's help and journal what he shows you.

Simmering anger ....

....

Jealousy ....

....

Insecurity ....

....

Using other people to prop yourself up ....

....

Hopelessness ....

....

Rage ....

....

Perfectionism ....

....

How do you need to "hold and fold" in this situation? How will you let God be God in your life?

....

....

....

....

....

....

What to Do with Shame

Add the character names to replace the pronouns in Genesis 16:6:

Then _____ dealt harshly with _____ and

_____ fled from _____.

I loathe this scene where a woman is abusing power and lashing out physically. I hate that it's included in my Bible, but I'm also very thankful. Why? Because I have my own scenes of shameful behavior; there are times when my name could go in blanks like those. I look back on the instances where I've lashed out in anger and pain—trying to control some person I love or some outcome I couldn't live without, and I am grieved with deep sorrow and regret.

Do you have shameful moments that you regret, too? What should we *do* with the shame?

I remember a particular night that was chock-full of sin in the Popkin household. I had been engrossed in a project, dinner was late, and everyone was hungry, grumpy, and short-tempered. At about eight o'clock, Ken barked the order for everyone to just go to bed. "Aren't we going to do Bible time?" I asked, pulling out the gospel booklet we had been working through with the kids.

He said, "This night has been awful. The last thing I want to do is talk about the gospel."

"But haven't we all just demonstrated how desperately we need it?" I asked. He reluctantly agreed, and we gathered the kids to the family room, where Ken used an illustration about our heavy backpacks full of sin, which can only be emptied at the cross. That was the night our sweet seven-year-old, Cade, gave his life to Jesus.

Sister, the best thing sinful, shame-filled people can do is run to the cross! Run to the gospel, every day and every hour! The more brutally honest we are about our shameful, control-craving behavior, the more relevant God's promises become.

Sarai's and Hagar's story of tangled jealousy, self-focus, white-knuckled control, greed, abuse, callousness, and violence never should have happened. But it did. And every detail—both in this story and our own—displays our desperate need for the gospel. Our only hope is the story God was writing when he promised Abram and Sarai a son.

A Sinful Mother

Take one more moment and seat yourself among the Wildernites, considering this story through their eyes. They had endured centuries of slavery. The Egyptians treated them so harshly, that—like Hagar—they had to flee.

And here they were—proof that God keeps his promises. It was from their family line that the promised offspring and Savior of the world would be born. Yet, this story makes it clear: God didn't choose them because of their righteous living. Their *foremother*, of all people, had been just as harsh and abusive as their slave owners! So what does this mean for the Wildernites and us?

God's promises are not contingent on our ability to not sin; God's promises are in *response* to our sin. Sarai was only confirming—along with the rest of humanity—how much she too needed the promised offspring and Savior. We have waded through some ugly scenes from Sarai's life, and yet we haven't seen God write Sarai out of the story. We'll only see him faithfully fulfilling his promises.

Now, Sarai's story will offer us plenty of consequences to avoid, yet she did not and *could* not thwart the plans of the God who says, "I will." Nor can you. One of our most precious promises is that God will make us righteous like him. Oh, how I long for that day!

Briefly share about a sin you feel most chained to or ashamed of. Does it have anything to do with control?

....

....

....

....

....

In Christ, what is true of you, according to 2 Corinthians 5:21?

....

....

....

....

....

Rewrite 2 Timothy 2:13 using a first-person point of view.

If I am ... .

....

....

....

....

....

....

Considering Him Faithful

Check your timeline on page 17 and add chapter titles below:

Genesis 12: ....

....

    Sarai's age: ....

Genesis 15: ....

....

Genesis 16: ....

....

    Sarai's age: ....

By year ten, our walk-by-faith pioneer woman is living more like a walk-by-faith dropout. However, this part of her story gives us a chance to consider and cherish God's faithfulness despite our faithlessness.

RETELL

Summarize the story of Sarai's plan to staple fruit onto the family tree, and include these quotes:

"The Lord has prevented me from bearing children." (Genesis 16:2)

"Go, sleep with my slave; perhaps I can build a family through her." (Genesis 16:2 NIV)

"May the wrong done to me be on you!" (Genesis 16:5)

"Do whatever you want with her." (Genesis 16:6 CSB)

....

....

....

....

....

....

....

....

....

....

....

....

....

....

....

....

....

REFLECT

Review some key points from the week and reflect on how God is inviting you to respond.

Sarai got impatient. She didn't want to wait on God to produce the fruit on her brittle branch. And yet, whether on fruit trees or family trees, God makes the fruit grow. He is the Creator. Fruitfulness of any form is a gift from him.

In what situations have you tried to "staple up fruit" of your own making, and why? How are self-reliance and faith incompatible?

....

....

....

What spiritual fruit do you see on your own branches? (Check the list in Galatians 5:22–23.) How is this a result of God's faithfulness to you?

....

....

....

....

Sarai was talking, and Abram was listening—not to God, but to her. As wives, sometimes we need to stop talking so our husbands can hear from God.

What have you been trying to talk your husband (or someone else) into? What will you stop talking about and start praying about?

....

....

....

Brainstorm a list of ways you can show your support of husbands leading their families (either your own or someone else's). I'll give you a couple of examples to get you started.

Say to my husband: I'll support you either way.

Ask my friend: What does your husband think?

....

....

....

....

....

....

Sarai was trying to build herself up with a baby, but things teetered in the opposite direction when Hagar humiliated her. Then when Abram was passive, Sarai turned her rage on Hagar and lost control of the only person who was hers to control: herself.

How have your attempts to lift yourself up teetered in the wrong direction?

....

....

....

Note any recent instances of your seething anger, boiling-over rage, bitterness, perfectionism, anxiety, or fear. How is each the result of trying to control something you can't?

....

....

....

....

How is God asking you to "hold and fold" in at least one situation?

....

....

....

REHEARSE

As Sarai lashes out with crass language, wounded anger, and abusive rage, amazingly, she is not disqualified from God's promises. She only demonstrates how desperately she needs the Savior that God has promised.

How is this part of Sarai's story a warning against self-reliance and control? How does this story highlight God's faithfulness?

....

....

....

Will you be shaped by God's promises? Choose a meaningful promise from page 291, along with a verse to memorize. Write them both below.

....

....

....

....

....

....

....

Renewed Hope

Renewed Hope

New Names

When my daughter Lindsay was two years old, my mom carried her into a store to pick up an order. The woman at the counter asked for Mom's name, and she said, "Judie." Then Lindsay used her chubby hands to turn Mom's face to her, and asked, incredulously, "You name is *Judie*?"

Lindsay couldn't fathom that her "Mamaw" had a name she had never heard of.

As we dive back into Sarai's story, God is going to reintroduce himself to Abram with a different name and unveil some new names for Abram and Sarai as well.

The God Who Sees

It's now been thirteen years since Sarai treated Hagar so harshly that she fled into the wilderness. It's been thirteen years since God met Hagar there and had a conversation with her. Unfortunately, we won't have time to carefully consider Hagar's wilderness story (she deserves a study of her own!), but let's consider it through Sarai's eyes.

What did God say to Hagar in Genesis 16:10?

....

....

....

How was this similar to what God said to Abram in Genesis 15:5?

....

....

Who was and wasn't mentioned at Ishmael's birth in Genesis 16:15? Why do you suppose this is?

....

....

....

Would Sarai have likely presumed that Hagar's son was the son God promised? Why or why not?

....

....

....

How does God describe what Ishmael will become in Genesis 16:12?

....

....

....

Imagine thirteen-year-old Ishmael, beginning to fit this description. How might this have affected Sarai?

....

....

....

When God met Hagar at that well, he promised her baby would grow up to be like a wild donkey. Wild donkeys aren't bound; they're free, so you can imagine what hope this gave Hagar. Afterward, Hagar named God "El-roi," or "The God Who Sees"—and apparently she came back talking about it because the well was then named after her encounter (Genesis 16:14).

So, how do you think Sarai felt about Hagar's encounter with "The God Who Sees"? Perhaps she felt guilty about God seeing *her*. Sarai had used Hagar, then harshly mistreated her. But God treated Hagar tenderly and promised her more offspring than she could count.

As Sarai watched Ishmael grow into that wild donkey of a teenage boy, it looked like she was being passed over and left out. It seemed like the story had moved on without her. And yet there was still so much for Sarai to learn about the God who says, "I will."

Reintroduction

Read Genesis 17:1–8.

What new name for himself does God share with Abram? Can you find out what the name means?

....

....

Briefly list the things God says he will do:

I will ....

I will ....

    And ....

I will ....

I will ....

I will ....

Put a check mark next to any of these that will happen for future generations, after Abram is gone.

When You Think God Needs Help

Suppose my husband goes to move a fifty-pound object and I say, "Oh, babe . . . that's really heavy. Want me to call someone to give you a hand?" Worse yet, suppose I try to move it *for* him. He would say, "You don't think I can move fifty pounds?" And then, "If you did, why did you think I needed a hand?"

By trying to "help God out," Abram (and Sarai) have treated God as if he needs a hand, so God is here to set the record straight. I think I hear a bit of correction in God's tone as he tells Abram, "I'm the God who is strong and able. My name is God Almighty." You see, he knows we can't be shaped by the promises of a God we think needs our help.

The God who says, "I will" reminds Abram of his covenant promises—specifically the ones he will keep to Abram's descendants in the centuries to come—long after Abram is able to "help out." The point is: God is eternally able to do as he has promised.

New Names

God not only introduces his own new name, he gives new names to Abram and Sarai as well. In the West, we don't put as much emphasis on a name's meaning, but in the Middle East your name is something you grow into or become. I heard about a tour guide in Israel whose name meant "generous," and he said, "I am always looking for ways to be generous and live up to my name."

Read Genesis 17:3-6.

How would Abram live up to his new name's meaning (v. 5)?

....

....

....

....

How old is Abram (approximately) at this point? Check your time-line on page 17.

....

What new information does God give about the promised offspring in verses 6 and 16 of chapter 17?

....

....

....

Read Genesis 17:15-16.

What new name and new information is given about Sarai?

....

....

....

In Matthew 1:2-16, how does Matthew begin and end his genealogy? How does this emphasize the importance of Sarah's offspring?

....

....

....

What king is mentioned in the genealogy?

....

....

God adds the Hebrew letter "Hey" (which sounds like our "H") to both Sarah and Abraham's new names. Some rabbis teach that—like when Psalm 33:6 says that God made the heavens "by the breath of his mouth"—God is breathing his supernatural creative power into Abraham and Sarah's names.[1]

Abram means, "exalted father." Abraham means, "father of nations." That first name was something he could "live up to" without outside help. After all, Ishmael called him "father" or "daddy," right? But father of nations? That's not something Abraham could grow himself into without God's help.

Sarai and Sarah both mean "princess." Royal princesses are the ones who become mamas to kings, right? All along, God has known that Sarai would not only become a mother, but also the mother of the line leading to Jesus—the King of Kings.

With these new names, God was signaling a change coming. And notice: Sarah is part of it.

Over the past thirteen years, Sarah has never been excluded from God's plans. She hasn't been brushed aside or passed over; she only *thought* she had been. All along, Sarah has been tucked inside God's parentheses as a princess, mother of kings.

When God Came to Lunch

Following God is a group activity; we need each other on this faith journey. But we respond to God as individuals—those sweet moments where the God of the universe sits with us and invites our faith. Today's lesson is about the moment Sarah got to hear directly from God.

Hospitable Abraham

Read Genesis 18:1–8.

Find several verbs that describe Abraham's actions. What is his attitude toward the visitors?

....

....

....

Do you think Abraham knows this is the Lord? Support your answer from the text.

....

....

....

As Abraham enjoys his noonday siesta, out of nowhere, three visitors appear. Apparently, they can tell which tent belongs to the head of the clan, and by approaching they indicate their wish to be Abraham's guests.[2]

Abraham greets them and rushes around with preparations, then serves them under a tree. Abraham clearly recognized that these were honorable guests. He just didn't know *how* honorable, until something was said at the dinner table.

A Table Conversation

Consider the dialogue in Genesis 18:9–10.

What did the visitors ask Abraham, and why was this surprising (v. 9)?

....

....

Who is speaking in verse 10? To whom?

....

....

What is Sarah doing (v. 10)?

....

....

How does the visitor's promise in verse 10 compare with the promise given to Abraham in Genesis 17:21?

....

....

How much time do you think passed between these two promises, and why?

....

....

....

A Long Overdue Date

Picture someone in her late eighties saying, "I'm hoping for a baby." You might think she needed a cognitive evaluation, right? For this reason, I doubt Abraham and Sarah spoke publicly about their hope for a baby. And yet, the visitor at their table not only brings up this God-inspired dream, he offers them a timestamped promise.

Sister, here it is. The moment we've been waiting for. God just dropped the bombshell by restating the promise with the detail Sarah has been longing for: *when*. This time next year she'll be holding an infant! So, um . . . did everyone just hear? Why aren't they group-hugging? Why aren't tears flowing? Why is everybody just sitting there? Could it be they don't really believe what God said? I'll be generous and assume they are just stunned.

Both last time (Genesis 17:21) and this time (Genesis 18:10), God says the baby will come, "a year from now," so these must be back-to-back conversations. And last time, Abraham was circumcised that same day—so he probably wouldn't have been running to meet visitors for a bit. (I'm surprised, at ninety-nine, that he's running at all.) My best guess: A week or so has passed. And why has God returned so soon? He gave us a hint when he asked about Sarah by name.

God's Friend

My friend Katlin recently found a bag on her front porch with a tract from an organization that often goes door-to-door. Inside were beautiful handcrafted baskets—but when she saw her kids' names embroidered on the front, it felt invasive and uncomfortable. *How did they know our names?* she wondered.

Later, Katlin laughed when she learned that the baskets were a gift—not from the door-to-door visitors, but from a trusted friend. They just happened to be dropped off the same day.

When God asked about Abraham's wife by name—especially her *new* name—perhaps it did make Abraham feel uncomfortable for a moment. If it hadn't dawned on him already, this was Abraham's clue that the visitors at his table were not ordinary guests.

In lesson 1, the Lord reintroduced himself as God Almighty; but in this visit, he stops by as a friend. Sister, God Almighty knows your name, your kids' names, and the name of your neighbor's cat. But don't let that make you uncomfortable, because he comes as a friend.

How is James 2:23 displayed in this story?

How is our perspective skewed if we know the Lord as "God Almighty" (Genesis 17:1), but never as friend?

How is our perspective skewed if we know the Lord as friend, but never God Almighty?

Do you know the Lord as God Almighty, as friend, or both? What difference does it make that he knows your name?

Visits to the Abrahams

At this point, God has visited a number of times. See if you can give the answer from memory:

Whom did God visit? Circle A: Abraham, S: Sarah, H: Hagar

Genesis 12:1–3	A S H	**Genesis 16:7–14**	A S H
Genesis 12:6–7	A S H	**Genesis 17:1–22**	A S H
Genesis 15	A S H	**Genesis 18:1–10**	A S H

Abraham got to see smoking firepots and go stargazing with God. Hagar was rescued by God, who gave her prophecies about her future. And Sarah got to hear about it all, secondhand.

Obviously, Sarah knew about Abraham's recent encounter with God. (The circumcision day wasn't something you'd forget.) But had Abraham revealed *all* that God said, including the time-stamped birth announcement from God?

Maybe Abraham wanted to protect Sarah from getting her hopes up. Or maybe he knew she wouldn't believe. It's not clear, but this is: God is at Abraham's table, purposefully delivering a message to the one listening in the tent.

Individual Attention from God

Picture God tearing some of Sarah's hot-off-the-coals bread, dipping it in butter, then asking, "Where's your wife? Where's Sarah?" Knowing she's behind him, God uses her name to get her attention. He wants Sarah to overhear the promise from his very lips.

It's one thing to know about God and the story he's writing. It's another thing to see yourself *in* the story and encounter the living God. I imagine Sarah returned to this memory of God eating her bread and asking for her by name hundreds of times. Can you imagine how meaningful it was? Especially after thirteen years of wondering whether she had either messed up God's plan or disqualified herself from being useful to him.

God Almighty was at her table, tenderly seeking her out. He had shown up for *her*.

Sister, God also shows up for *you*. Do you realize that you too are part of his story? Don't make the mistake of thinking you can mess up God's plans. You can't! And don't doubt whether you are relevant to his story. You are! Perhaps God wants to spend a moment at your table today, assuring you of his promises and inviting you to be shaped by them in the coming year.

The words on God's lips were meant for Sarah, as she listened in. And the words in your Bible are just as assuredly meant for you. God wants you to regularly settle yourself, like a woman on the other side of the tent flap, ready to "overhear" the promises he speaks from the thin pages of your Bible. He wants you to know he was thinking of you when he made them.

How does this story correct any wrong ideas you've had about feeling irrelevant or excluded from God's plans?

....

....

....

Tell of a time God supernaturally used the pages of your Bible to give you assurance or hope.

....

....

....

....

....

How will you make more time to listen in to God's promises?

....

....

....

....

....

....

....

....

....

....

Old and Worn Out

Alone in the green room before speaking at a women's event, I took advantage of the solitude. I got on my knees before the Lord and poured out my heart, in anguish over the way I had behaved earlier that day. "I'm so sorry, Lord! I'm so ashamed of how selfish I was. How can you possibly use someone like me? I feel so inadequate!"

It's not a prayer I would have spoken out loud if I'd known anyone could hear me—especially not anyone from the church that had hired me to serve the women who were at that moment filing into the sanctuary. It wasn't until after I reapplied mascara and stepped out of the green room that I realized (with horror) that the microphone I was wearing was on.

I never asked the tech booth guys if they had overheard my private green room prayers. I didn't want to know. I simply left my prayer with God and received his flooding assurance of forgiveness and grace. Then I stepped onto the platform, where God was kind enough to use me— even me—to accomplish his purposes that evening.

This page in our Bibles is sort of like my live mic—giving access to some words that Sarah probably never would have shared if she knew anyone was listening in.

Worn Out, Worn Through

Read Genesis 18:9–15.

Where is Sarah? Describe the scene.

....

....

....

What message does Sarah laugh in response to (v. 10)?

....

....

So Sarah laughed to herself. (Genesis 18:12)

Circle the connector word, "so."

What two details does the narrator include in the previous verse?

....

....

Check your timeline on page 17. How old are Abraham and Sarah at this point?

....

Write out Sarah's private thought, recorded for us in Genesis 18:12:

....

....

....

Sarah has apparently reached menopause, so when she overhears this visitor say, "Sarah's going to have a baby next year," she laughs. Apparently, this visitor hasn't seen her wrinkles and gray hair. And clearly, he doesn't know that after decades of infertility, her hope of motherhood has completely expired.

The phrase Sarah uses to describe herself is not kind:

After I am _____ _____ and my lord is old . . . . (Genesis 18:12)

How is this same phrase used in the following passages?

Deuteronomy 29:5 ....

....

Job 13:28 ....

....

Lamentations 3:4 ....

....

Sarah is describing herself like an old cloth, too worn to even keep as a cleaning rag. Now, perhaps she wouldn't say this out loud, but even our self-talk matters to God.

What do you think triggered Sarah's negative self-talk?

....

....

What topics or contexts trigger your negative self-talk?

....

....

In what ways do you feel like your life is "worn out" or purposeless?

....

....

What insight do you find in 2 Corinthians 4:16?

....

....

....

....

....

Sarah's Sex Life

I've never loved the fact that there's a transom window above our bedroom door, but especially so the day I found a barstool outside our bedroom. I asked my nine-year-old about it and he said, "Oh, I didn't want to wake you and daddy, so I was trying to see if you were up."

I said, "Honey, you can't look through that window. Sometimes mommy is changing clothes in there." He looked horrified, and I was glad; I didn't want to worry about what else he might see through that window.

Most of the women I know are pretty private about their periods and sex lives. We certainly wouldn't want God publishing any of our details in his eternal book, but that's exactly what happens to Sarah. Look at the second thing Sarah says to herself:

> **After I am worn out, and my lord is old, shall I have _____?**
> **(Genesis 18:12)**

This Hebrew word refers to sexual pleasure, not (as you may have assumed) the pleasure of becoming a mom.[3] So Sarah is giving us a glance through her "transom window," where there's nothing happening behind locked doors. Or to put it bluntly, the Abrahams are no longer having sex.

You might be thinking, "And why did God think it necessary that I know this?" Well, as it turns out, it's a pretty important detail. Because as you might know, sex is necessary to have a baby. And if Abraham and Sarah aren't having sex anymore, they're going to need to start. (More on that later.)

When a woman feels worthless and inadequate (as Sarah does), she often pulls back from relationships in self-protectiveness. And for Sarah, "the other woman" is still putting a strain on her marriage. Fortunately, though, the greatest marriage expert of all time is at the table, ready to help.

God Questions

Look again at Genesis 18:13–15.

What questions does God ask, and why does he ask them?

....

....

....

....

What do you think God wants Sarah to reconsider?

....

....

....

....

What can you learn about God's interaction with you?

....

....

....

....

Why did she laugh? Well, the answer is obvious, considering she's almost ninety years old. Sarah is too old to have a baby. But then, this is *God* saying she *will*. The One who created wombs and seed and motherhood and families is the same One who is promising Sarah a baby—and even giving her a due date! But Sarah scoffs, because this is inconceivable to her. She's still learning who God is.

There's a direct correlation between how we see God and how we view the future. A small view of God says, "Well, he can't do much," or "He doesn't see, he doesn't care." Like Sarah, we slip into despondency about our own limitations. Even when God is sitting at the table, blessing us with some outlandish promise, we can't see it. But when we stop and ponder who God is and consider what he has done, the horizon stretches and our view of God widens. We're able to face even the grimmest of circumstances, saying, "My God can do anything!"

Gaby's Big God

Twenty-seven-year-old Gaby has already experienced many of cancer's losses: What she looks like. What she eats. What people think of her. With her new medication (as I shared earlier), there's a loss of probability that Gaby will have children. These losses are painful. Crushing. But Gaby's big view of God keeps her from despair.

Listen to more of Gaby Puente's story on Shannon's Live Like It's True podcast. Go to shannonpopkin.com /promises.

Gaby is convinced God can heal her and give her a family someday if he chooses. And if he doesn't, she's convinced God will grow her faith and bring glory to himself. Ultimately, Gaby believes God's promises about his Garden City with its unshakable foundations. She will walk its streets with a body that is forever whole. She will feast at God's table, surrounded by family—including those she has spiritually mothered. She will be filled with joy in God's presence and live eternally, experiencing pleasures forevermore (Psalm 16:11). If God is able to give Gaby all of this, he's able to do anything!

He Is Able

Sarah might see herself as worthless and worn out, but God does not—and the most important thing about us is not what we see, but what God does. God has appointed Sarah for a role in his great rescue operation that offers sweeping hope to all mankind. She is essential to the plan, but for Sarah to play this role, she must believe this truth: God is able to do *anything*. And he *must* keep his promises.

Wonder-Infused Laughter

When Granny Ryan (my mom's grandmother) was out working in the field one day, she saw a Goodyear blimp in the sky and—since she had never seen such a thing—she mistook it for Jesus. Granny went tearing into the house, quickly trying to change clothes. When somebody asked what was going on, she said, "The Lord's come back, and here I am in these pants!"

Don't you love her sense of anticipation? She sees something foreign in the sky and her first thought is, *Jesus has come!* Granny Ryan was a woman shaped by God's promises.

Sadly, Sarah is not. Even after God has explicitly stated (we assume Abram shared this news with her) that Sarah will bear Abram's child, any anticipation of God keeping his promises is rather absent in her.

Read Genesis 18:9–15.

When God quotes Sarah, is his recounting of her words accurate? Compare verses 12 and 13.

....

What does God's question in verse 14 have to do with the news of Sarah's due date?

....

....

....

Whom does God address in verse 13, then in verse 15? What has shifted?

....

....

....

Compare Sarah's laughter with Abraham's laughter in Genesis 17:17–19.

    What are the similarities?

....

....

    Do you detect any differences?

....

....

How is God's response different?

....

....

Read Romans 4:19–21.

How do the facts affect Abraham's faith?

....

....

....

What happened to Abraham's faith and how (vv. 20–21)?

....

....

....

What can we learn about faith from Abraham?

....

....

....

....

....

The Laughter of Faith

Remember the water polo window under the surface? Genesis gives us a broad view from the bleachers, but in Romans 4, we get a deeper, "underwater" view of Abraham's faith.

Sarah, having a baby at age ninety? Abraham can't help but laugh (Genesis 17:17). And yet, his laughter is tempered by faith.[4] While Sarah is focused on how she feels about herself and what she sees in the mirror, Abraham is focused on what he knows about *God*. Reflecting on Romans 4:17, which says Abraham believed God could create something from nothing, Tim Keller imagines Abraham reasoning, "[God is] the One who hung the sun and moon and scattered the stars like sand with both hands! It is ridiculous for me to think our age presents such a being with an obstacle."[5]

This faith, however, was the missing ingredient in Sarah's laughter, and God calls her out on it. Don't you love, though, how God skips the embarrassing parts of Sarah's self-talk? His purpose isn't to shame her, but to gently confront her. And by the end of the dialogue, did you notice that rather than talking *about* Sarah, he's talking *to* her? Perhaps he turned to make eye contact as she peeked through the tent flap. Or maybe she was called out to face this divine visitor. Either way, God is not too polite to confront Sarah's doubt. He asks:

Is anything _____ _____ for the LORD? (Genesis 18:14)

Coffee-Spitting Doubt

In a GIF I saw recently of a woman doubled over, spitting out her coffee, I could tell two things: she thought something was funny, and she also thought it was ludicrous. That's how I hear Sarah laughing in this text.

Sarah has spent so much time doubting that God's promises apply to her, she can't even conceive of the possibility. She's spitting out her coffee at the very idea of becoming pregnant, and her despondent laughter is quite telling. It's a sure sign that she is being shaped not by God's promises, but by her doubts. So God poses a question, directed at her heart.

Your Bible might read, "Is anything too hard for the LORD?" (Genesis 18:14), but the Hebrew word is better captured by the translation "wonderful."[6] God is asking, "Is there anything too wonderful for me to do? If not, where is your wonder, Sarah?"

Picture that moment when you get news that is incredulously true:
The cancer is gone!
The prodigal has come home!
The marriage is reconciled!
The treatment worked!
The missing child has been found!

God has delivered a message just as wonderful as any of these—and more so! Very soon, the pregnancy test will be positive, and Sarah will hold the promised offspring in her arms. The first descendant in a line leading to the Savior will be born.

Another Miracle Baby

Centuries later, another heavenly visitor visits another woman with a birth announcement for the promised offspring, Jesus. Take a moment to read Luke 1:26–38 and notice the similarities. For Mary, it's much too soon to have a baby. For Sarah, it's much too late. But in both instances, a heavenly being says, "Nothing will be impossible with God" (Luke 1:37 CSB).

Notice the difference, though, in the women's responses. Mary asks openly, "How can this be?" (Luke 1:34 CSB) then responds in beautiful surrender, saying, "May it happen to me as you have said" (Luke 1:38 CSB). But Sarah conceals her doubts, saying, "I did not laugh," then has no comment about the promised birth (Genesis 18:15).

It's worth mentioning that Mary is young and Sarah is old. Have you noticed how easy it is for children to be filled with wonder? But as we age, time has a way of siphoning our wonder. Many of us can look back on moments when our radical obedience was fueled by hope for God's favor. But then, as the calendar pages turn or the age spots accumulate, disappointment tends to drain that hope. The long stretch between the parentheses gives ample space for doubt to crescendo into a roar. Over time, our doubts silence faith's wonder.

He's too stubborn to change.
He's too old to find purpose.
There's no hope for this marriage.
She's been addicted for far too long.
The cancer has spread too far.
He's been a prodigal for too many years.

Confronting Doubt

I don't know about you, but when I see a woman—especially an elderly one—who is so utterly disappointed with God, I am hesitant to remind her of his promises. To open my Bible seems preachy. To confront her despondence seems harsh. And yet God does not hesitate. Our God does not consider it inconsiderate or harsh when he invites us to reject our doubts and be shaped by his promises.

For each pair, mark the correct version from Genesis 18:13–15:

___ The LORD said to Abraham, "Why did Sarah laugh?"
___ The LORD said to Sarah, "Why did you laugh?"

___ The LORD asked, "Why did Sarah say, 'Shall I indeed bear a child, now that I am old?'"
___ The LORD asked, "Why did Sarah say, 'Shall I have intimacy with my husband, now that I'm worthlessly decrepit and old?'"

___ The LORD said, "Is anything too wonderful for God? This time next year, Sarah shall have a son." And Sarah laughed in wonder, and said, "I am the LORD's servant!"
___ The LORD said, "Is anything too wonderful for God? This time next year, Sarah shall have a son." And Sarah denied it, saying, "I didn't laugh."

___ The LORD said, "No, but she did laugh."
___ The LORD said, "No, but you did laugh."

God has just given Sarah the equivalent of a trillion-dollar check, and she's laughing at the possibility of it being anything more than paper. But why? Does she believe that the eternal, Almighty God is unable to keep his promise? Does she not believe that he is faithful? Those are good questions for us to consider as well.

Sister, do you anticipate that God will keep his promises the way Granny Ryan did? Do you look up at the sky, knowing that Jesus will return? The reality is, God has given *you* the equivalent of a trillion-dollar check. Can you even put a price on his friendship? His forgiveness? Your hope of being raised from the dead? Eternity in paradise? If you, like Sarah, have allowed doubt to swell like a crescendo in your head, God is not too polite to confront your doubts.

Which situation most tempts you to doubt God? Does something seem too impossible? Is it taking too long?

....

....

....

How is your faith in response to this situation limited by your feelings about yourself or your circumstances?

....

....

....

How might a sense of wonder over what God could do in this situation require faith?

....

....

....

How is God using Sarah's story to confront your doubts or lack of faith?

....

....

....

A Wonder-Full Story

God not only gives us stories in the Bible, but stories today that stir up wonder in our hearts. Here's a wonder-filled story that I got to be part of.

Our neighbor Warren was an elderly man who was very opposed to the gospel. Whenever we stopped to talk with Warren or had him over for dinner, we would try to bring up spiritual matters, but Warren was skeptical. He thought the Bible was just an old book and Jesus was just a good teacher. He doubted if God was even real, and he certainly didn't want God telling him what to do. So our conversations about the good news of Jesus didn't go very far. Or so we thought.

One day we saw a moving truck in Warren's driveway, and we learned that Warren had been moved to a memory care facility. When we went to visit him, Warren didn't recognize us and was agitated. But when we visited again, the nurse said, "You've come on a good day!"

When we walked in Warren said, "I was wondering when you were going to come see me!" He asked us to share the gospel with him, and we were delighted to do so. It felt like holy ground there beside his bed, as Warren cried over decades of hard-hearted sin, asked God for forgiveness, and confessed his belief in God's promises. It was a thing of wonder!

Warren never recognized us again after that night. I think God cleared the cobwebs from his mind and gave him a day of clarity because he wanted to bless Warren with eternal life. We moved away soon after and never got to share that story with Warren's loved ones. I've often wondered if anyone will be surprised to see Warren in heaven. His story begs the question: is anything too wonderful for God?

Is Anything Too Wonderful?

Those of us who know God have no business living without wonder. I'm not talking about Pollyanna optimism; I'm talking about trusting in a God who says, "Is anything to wonderful for me?"

This God of ours promises that great sinners will be washed clean and made unable to sin. He promises that people will rise from their graves and be given bodies that won't die. He promises he'll dwell to-gether with us—his friends—on a re-Edenized planet.

When we doubt God's promises, it's not because they seem too small to do much good; it's because they seem too good to be true.

Respond to that last statement. How is this true of you?

....

....

....

How did Warren's story resonate with you? Do you have any wonder-full stories? How might your story encourage someone else who is struggling with doubt?

....

....

....

What are you hoping God will do in this lifetime that would be amazing?

....

....

....

What amazing thing do you believe God will do, in keeping with his promises?

....

....

....

Sister, you have no business living without wonder, because all of God's audacious promises to you are going to come true.

Considering Him Faithful

Look back at your timeline on page 17.

How many years have now lapsed since God made his first promises to Abram?

....

How many years have passed since Ishmael's birth?

....

Add Sarah's age and chapter titles to the following:

Genesis 12: ....

....

....

Genesis 16: ....

....

....

Genesis 18: ....

....

....

For thirteen years, Sarah's doubts have been growing. So much so, she responds to the visitor's prediction of her pregnancy with despondent laughter. Yet God had come to stir up wonder in Sarah. What he had promised in the first place, he was about to do. It was time for Sarah to be shaped by God's promises.

RETELL

Summarize the story of God coming to lunch, include these quotes:

"Where is Sarah your wife?" (Genesis 18:9)

"In about a year's time … your wife Sarah will have a son!" (Genesis 18:10 csb)

"After I am worn out, and my lord is old, shall I have pleasure?" (Genesis 18:12)

"Why did Sarah laugh?" (Genesis 18:13)

"Is anything too wonderful for the Lord?" (Genesis 18:14)

....

....

....

....

....

....

....

....

....

....

....

REFLECT

Review some key points from the week and reflect on how God is inviting you to respond.

Would you like a place behind the tent flap to overhear God restating his promises that apply to you? In a sense, that's what you're doing as you read your Bible. The promises on its pages, written for the people of God are for you, and God wants you to know he was thinking of you when he made them.

Tell about a time God used the Bible to reassure you of his promises.

....

....

....

How often do you read your Bible? Do you open it hoping to hear from God? What adjustments will you make?

....

....

When the visitor says Sarah will have a baby, she laughs and her self-talk gives us a window into her heart. Sarah feels old and worthless; she's no longer being shaped by God's promises.

What situations tend to trigger feelings of worthlessness in you about yourself or hopelessness about your future? Review 2 Corinthians 4:16. How does this give you hope?

....

....

....

....

Spend five minutes in deliberate thought about God. List what you know about him based on Bible stories you've read. Record how this shifts your perspective about yourself.

....
....
....
....
....

Record a plan to stop, ponder God, and widen your view of him the next time you feel worthless or hopeless:

....
....
....
....

God is not too polite to confront Sarah's doubts which have grown like a crescendo. He kindly asks her to be shaped by his promises, asking, "Is anything too wonderful for the LORD?"

How is doubt or skepticism similar to saying, "This is too wonderful, even for God"?

....
....
....
....
....
....
....

Which situation today most tempts you to doubt God? Write out a request to God that requires wonder, then write in all capital letters: IS ANYTHING TOO WONDERFUL FOR GOD?

....

....

....

....

....

....

....

....

....

....

REHEARSE

In this story, God shows up to remind Sarah that he is still the faithful God who will keep his promises. He makes the promises. He keeps the promises. And he invites her to believe that the promises will come true.

How do you see God's faithfulness to Sarah in this story?

....

....

....

....

....

Will you be shaped by God's promises? Choose a meaningful promise from appendix 2 (page 291), along with a verse to memorize. Write them both below.

....

....

....

....

....

....

....

....

....

....

....

....

....

....

Reverting to Fear

Reverting to Fear

Sister Act II

After thirteen years of watching the wind blow and Ishmael grow into a difficult teen, God appears to Abraham (Genesis 17) and puts a time stamp on his promise: Sarah will have a son this time next year. Soon after, God shows up at lunch (Genesis 18) and repeats the promise for Sarah to overhear. Then the storyline moves to another section which doesn't include Sarah, but affects her deeply.

Take a few minutes to read Genesis 18:16–33 and Genesis 19.

The Tragedy of Sodom

After dining with the three heavenly visitors, Abraham walks them to an overlook of Sodom and Gomorrah, where God confides his plan. He has come to investigate the outcry of the oppressed in these cities and do something about it. Abraham (thinking of Lot) intercedes, pleading that God not sweep away the righteous of Sodom with the wicked (Genesis 18:23). God agrees. If ten righteous can be found, he will spare Sodom.

But there are not even ten. When the two angels arrive in Sodom, Lot insists they stay in his home—which is soon surrounded by all the men of the city, who lustfully demand to "know" these visitors. The angels strike the crowd with blindness, snatch Lot inside, and issue evacuation orders. Lot's family flees just as God blasts the city with sulfur and fire. Lot's wife turns back and becomes a pillar of salt, and so only three escape—Lot and his daughters—to a nearby cave. There we learn that Lot's daughters aren't righteous either; thinking all hope of marriage is lost, they get Lot drunk and become pregnant by him. These sordid details are set in juxtaposition with Abraham's righteous intercession. He's on the mountain, talking to God as a friend; they're in a cave, corrupted by sin.

Another Move

Imagine Abraham returning to that lookout the next morning as smoke rose from the scorched cities. Surely it felt like the whole world had come unhinged. With this in the backdrop, let's consider the story we'll be studying.

Read Genesis 20:1–2.

Mark the locations in verse 1 on your map on page 18.

> **Whose territory is this (21:34) and why would that be significant to the Wildernites? (See Numbers 13:28–29.)**

....

....

....

> **What happened to Sarah, and what does this remind you of?**

....

....

....

> **How much time has probably gone by since God's lunch visit? Consult your timeline on page 17.**

....

Taken. Again.

The Bible doesn't say why Abraham and Sarah pulled up their tent pegs this time, but we can imagine. Maybe the sulfur from Sodom's demolition had contaminated the water. Perhaps trade was disrupted. Maybe it was too disheartening to stay.

One thing's for sure: this was catastrophic and jarring. It was unsettling. Then, when the Abrahams arrive in Gerar, something else traumatic happens: Sarah is taken again.

What? How could Abraham let this happen again?! I doubt it's any less terrifying to be taken the second time.

Read Genesis 12:10–15 and contrast with Genesis 20:1–2 and 11–13 (which we'll look at more carefully later).

What similarities do you see?

....

....

....

....

Why would the narrator choose this timing for the reveal in Genesis 20:13?

....

....

....

What promises is Abraham once again forgetting? See Genesis 12:1–3.

....

....

....

Deleting History

Remember my photo illustration? I would never say, "Here's a man I met today who is faithful," because faithfulness is demonstrated over time. It makes more sense to show you a photo of Ken and say, "He has been a faithful husband for twenty-six years."

For twenty-some years, God has demonstrated his faithfulness to Abraham and Sarah. Remember how God appeared when they arrived in Canaan? And how he rescued them in Egypt? Remember how they left Egypt wealthy? Repeatedly, God has blessed them and given them reason to trust that he will keep his promises. Yet Abraham is deleting their history and acting like he doesn't even know God—let alone know him as a close, faithful friend. Once again Abraham is focused on the threats, not his theology. He's thinking about what people are like, not what God is like. He's turning to self-reliance, not God-reliance. And as a result, Sarah is cast into another devastating, no-win situation.

Old Sins

Abraham probably didn't even have to call for a "rehearsal" of the Sister Act before they arrived in Gerar. The narrator wants us to know that this has been part of their routine from day one. This was an old sin, not a new one.

When we first open the door to deception, it's easier to open that door again. Sometimes we open the door so frequently, we don't even see it as sin anymore. But God does. He's the one person we can't deceive. And God will press us to deal with the disparity between who we are and how we're living.

Check your timeline on page 17. How long has Abraham walked with God?

Assuming that Sarah didn't have a choice in the matter (I don't think she did), how might she feel about Abraham's lie?

....

....

....

Think of God's perspective. Do you think this "sister act" is more offensive to him than the first? Why or why not?

....

....

....

What are the things you lie about? What does your integrity reveal about your view of God?

....

....

....

Is a practiced sin a more tempting sin? Why or why not?

....

....

....

....

Elevator, Not Escalator

Faith is more like an elevator than an escalator, which only moves in one direction. With an escalator, you get on and it either carries you up or down. But an elevator has far more possibilities. You might get on and be carried up one floor, then down two, then up again. You can get out at any point and choose not to go up any further.

Our faith, like an elevator, rises and falls—but based on what? According to Tim Keller, "Faith is thinking about God, focusing on facts about him . . . [Faith is] a profound insistence on acting out of measured reflection instead of just reacting to circumstances."[1] When we focus on God or our circumstances, our faith rises and falls accordingly—and we take other people with us.

When Abraham was looking down on Sodom and pleading with God on their behalf, his faith was up in the penthouse. He was reverently appealing to God, both as his friend and the judge with sovereign power. But now, in just a matter of months if not weeks, Abraham's faith has plummeted to the basement. He's behaving as though there are no promises and no sovereign God. It's as if he has completely forgotten about his conversation with God over lunch a couple of weeks back. When you fail to think about God and reflect on his promises, you erase him from the scene just as Abraham has here. And then you have no one but yourself to rely on.

What difference does it make when you spend time carefully thinking about God?

....
....
....
....

When has your faith taken a basement plunge? Were you erasing God?

....
....
....
....

How have you been impacted by someone else's plunge to faith's basement?

....

....

....

....

When a Man of Faith Falls

My friend Jill Savage arrived home late one evening and found her husband asleep with his phone in his hand. When she went to plug it in, she saw some text messages that revealed Mark's secret affair with a woman from his past. Jill was sick to her stomach. Mark had been a pastor for twenty years; he knew the Lord. How could this be happening?

The next day when Jill confronted him, Mark said, "Yeah, I'm having an affair and I'm not stopping." Over the next few months, Mark waffled between his marriage and the affair, then decided to move out. Jill was left with the devastation of a disintegrating marriage of twenty-eight years.

During this difficult time, Jill's prayer became, "God, it's not well with my circumstances, but make it well with my soul." She chose to focus not on the mountain, but the Mountain Mover. Even as a child, Jill remembers reading "God stories" in her mom's Christian magazines, which seeded the idea that God can do *anything*. She believed that God was working and could heal her

Listen to more of Jill Savage's story on Shannon's Live Like It's True podcast. Go to shannonpopkin.com /promises.

marriage. But she didn't know if Mark would respond to God's rescue efforts. So Jill prayed and waited—believing that even if she didn't get the outcome she wanted, the wait was not wasted.

I'll tell you more about Jill's story later, but let's sit for a moment in the tension. Do you know a man of faith who has faltered? Perhaps your pastor, a Christian leader, or (like Jill) your own husband? Sister, I wish there was a verse in the Bible promising the outcome you want. What you have been given is a faithful God who invites you to look to him—believing that he can do *anything*. Will you turn to him in the waiting?

A Dead Man Walking

Read Genesis 20:1–7.

Notice the contrasts between Abraham in verse 2 and God in verse 3.

Abraham lied.

God ... .

....

....

Abraham made it seem like he wasn't married.

God ... .

....

....

Abraham made it seem like God wouldn't protect them.

God ... .

....

....

In verse 3, God told Abimelech he was a dead man because:

    a. He had slept with Sarah.

    b. Sarah was to be the mother of a new nation.

    c. He had taken another man's wife.

Who does God threaten to wipe out as collateral damage (vv. 4 and 7) and how does Genesis 19 make this _not_ an empty threat?

....

....

....

Is this the retribution you would expect from God? What is there to learn?

....

....

....

....

Kept from Sinning

Abraham might be tight-lipped about his marriage, but God sure isn't. His concern for his chosen people includes their reputations—and his own. God comes to Abimelech in a dream with both barrels loaded, saying, "You're a dead man. Sarah is already married."

Now, we can understand why Abimelech would argue his innocence since he didn't even know this marriage existed. In his defense, he hasn't slept with Sarah (Genesis 20:4), but God takes up an offense for Sarah anyway. So much so, he's threatening to bring death and destruction—and God doesn't make empty threats. (Just ask Sodom.)

Then God says something interesting:

Genesis 20:6 (csb) God says,

"I have also kept you from _____ against _____."

"I have not let you _____ her."

Rewrite these phrases, replacing the three pronouns (I, you, her) with their names (God, Sarah, and Abimelech). I'll get you started:

God kept Abimelech ....

....

....

If Abimelech had slept with Sarah, would this have been sin? Check your answer with verse 6.

....

....

....

List at least three things you learn about God in Genesis 20:6-7:

....

....

....

....

....

Do you hope God keeps you from sin? Do you have any examples of him doing so?

....

....

....

....

According to God, just because you don't have a guilty conscience, it doesn't mean you're not guilty of sin. Just like in Sodom and Gomorrah, God is the one who decides who is guilty and who is innocent.

From the first page of the Bible to the last, we learn that we cannot depend on ourselves to decide what is right or wrong, good or bad. We must defer to God.

He Must

But there's more to this story than meets the eye. This is not just a story about God protecting someone from sin; it's a story about the God who says, "I will."

Abimelech is a dead man walking because he has just tangled himself up in something more colossal than he could ever imagine. Without realizing it, he's just positioned himself to interfere with God's promises.

What did God promise:

> **in Genesis 17:21?** ....
>
> ....
>
> **in Genesis 18:14?** ....
>
> ....

Do the math. How much time does God have to keep this promise?

....

How is Abimelech posing a threat to God keeping his promise? How is this a threat to all of us who are "in Christ"?

....

....

....

....

Of all the families scattered across the globe, Abimelech has just dishonored the one family God has committed himself to protect. Of all the marriages in the world, Abimelech has just split up the one couple God has promised a miracle baby. Of all the women in the world, Abimelech has just taken the one woman God has given a due date in the coming year. As calendar pages turn and time slips by like desert sand through Sarah's fingers, there is no way God is going to let one little king keep him from doing all he has promised.

Since God's faithfulness is rooted in his own character, it is not possible for him to *not* fulfill his promises. He must! And he has.

Nothing Can Touch You

Sister, I hope this story makes you feel more safe and secure than ever before. Your God won't let anything stand in the way of him keeping his promises to you!

Now, I want to guard your heart against hurt and misunderstanding, so I'll say again: you and I are not promised safety from anything harmful touching us. (Even if I tried to promise that, you would know you couldn't believe me.)

The promise of safety in this story is tucked around Sarah, specifically. But there's a comforting promise for you tucked into Sarah's story as well. What's kept safe is Sarah's womb. What's kept safe is God's plan for salvation. What's kept safe is God's rock-solid commitment to provide a miracle baby, from which will come a nation, and then a Savior. What's kept safe is you, tucked in Christ.

If you are in Christ, from an eternal perspective, nothing, nothing, *nothing* can touch you.

The Right Kind of Fear

When my daughter was about twelve, I let her go to an amusement park with her friend's youth group, but the night before, I sat down with her to have a talk.

"Honey," I said. "It's very important that you stay with your friends tomorrow. I don't want you to split up for even a few minutes, okay?"

She said, "But what if they want to go on a ride that's too scary?" I told her she'd just have to do it. I explained that there are people who watch and wait for a moment when a young girl is alone, and even ventured a mild description of the horrors of sex trafficking. I didn't want to scare her, but I also didn't want her to be oblivious to what sinful people would like to take from her—from us.

Ken walked in just as tears welled up in our girl's eyes, and he asked what was going on. I said, "Well, I was just explaining to Lindsay about sex trafficking, and she's a little frightened."

"No," Lindsay said, her voice cracking. "That's not what I'm scared about." We both turned to her with obvious confusion. With tears spilling over, she said, "I'm afraid of going on those scary rides!"

Bless her heart. I was so grateful she had no idea what she was talking about. She was more frightened by being whipped upside down on an engineered-to-be-safe ride than by those who would tear her bubble-wrapped world to shreds.

Abraham wasn't naïve about the world. Glancing over his shoulder at a smoldering Sodom, he saw fresh evidence of how evil can corrupt an entire city—so that not even ten righteous people are left. But like my twelve-year-old, Abraham is confused about what to be scared of.

Read Genesis 20:1–13.

What questions does Abimelech have for Abraham?

....

....

....

What do Abraham's sin and excuses reveal about him?

....

....

....

What Abraham Saw

It's not wrong to be afraid of something. When my husband and I saw the spider and stopped, it was a healthy fear. But sometimes our fear becomes contorted—like when my daughter feared a roller coaster more than traffickers.

When our fear is skewed, so are our reactions. We either overreact or underreact. That's what Abimelech is getting at when he asks why Abraham did this terrible thing and lied that Sarah was his sister. The Hebrew literally translates, "What did you see?" (Genesis 20:10). In other words, he's asking, "How did we look to you? Why did you feel threatened? We're good people here! Why did you think you had to protect yourself?"

That's when Abraham reveals what he "saw" in Gerar that made him afraid. His combination of excuses is quite interesting. In Genesis 20:11 (CSB), Abraham said,

Excuse 1: "I thought, 'There is absolutely no

_____ of _____ in this place."

Excuse 2: "[I thought,] 'They will _____ me.'"

What irony do you see as you compare these two ideas?

....

....

....

....

Three Truths and a Fear

When Abraham arrives in Gerar, he's back to focusing on what people are like, not what God is like. We can imagine a hint of condescending disgust in Abraham's tone when he says, "There's absolutely no fear of God here." But is *Abraham* fearing God?

In her book, *Fight Your Fears*, my friend Kristen Wetherell says, "The root of our problem with fear isn't that we are too afraid, but that we aren't afraid enough of the God who is worthy to be feared."[2] If Abraham feared God (the way he claims the people of Gerar fail to), he wouldn't be bald-faced lying about his wife being his sister.

Now, Abraham lives in a world (as do we) where there *are* things to fear. It's a world in which two visitors arrive in town and are quickly surrounded by a city full of lustful men. It's a world in which a couple enters a town and the husband is quickly killed and his wife snatched. Abraham's fears are legitimate. But in his fear, he forgot God.

Kristen says, "We cannot deal with fear simply by choosing fearlessness. . . . What we need is an effective weapon with which to fight our fears. We need *truth*."³ Knowing who God is and what he has promised is the sword of truth that helps us do battle with fear.

What if Abraham had played, "Three Truths and a Fear"?

Truth: God is powerful. He destroyed a town with sulfur. (Genesis 19:24)
Truth: God promised to protect me. (Genesis 12:3)
Truth: God promised us a baby this year. (Genesis 17:21)
Fear: These people might kill me.

Do you see how the truths slice through the fear? We all have a choice. We can focus on the threats or our theology. We can focus on our fear of people or the promises of God.

Try a round of "Three Truths and a Fear." Choose truths about God or promises from his Word to fight one of your fears:

Truth: ....

Truth: ....

Truth: ....

Fear: ....

Abimelech's Influence

How quickly the threats can make us forget. Abraham knows the promises. He has observed God's faithfulness over decades. And yet he has inflated the people of Gerar so that they are the ones he fears. When we inflate people, we shrink God. When our fear of people gets big, our fear of God gets small. Ironically, Abimelech has more fear of God in this situation than *Abraham* does!

Look again at Genesis 20:8.

What effect does Abimelech have on his servants?

....

....

....

How does this show that Abraham was wrong about there being no fear of God in Gerar?

....

....

....

Abimelech prompts fresh fear of God to spread among his advisors. He surprises us with his correct fear of God's power and authority. Perhaps news of Sodom's sulfur and fire has reached him. Maybe he doesn't want to make the same mistake.

Even if he knows very little, Abimelech has a big view of God and a high regard for marriage. Ironically, Abraham doesn't. In Abraham's eyes, God is small and the people of Gerar are the ones to be feared.

Inflating People

Take your seat among the Wildernites as you consider this part of the story. Remember why they're in the wilderness? They are living out their forty-year consequence because rather than crossing the threshold into the promised land, they got scared.

Review what the scouts said about Canaan in Numbers 13:31–33.

What imagery do they use in verse 33 that tells us they felt small?

....

....

....

....

How did they inflate the people and shrink God?

....

....

....

The Wildernites were so close to seeing God close the parentheses and give them the promised land. But their fear made them forget God. The Canaanites looked so big; they forgot that God was bigger. Abraham and Sarah are in the same position. They're so close! God is just about to close the parentheses and give them a son.

Now, God hasn't asked Abraham and Sarah to pretend that the Canaanites in Gerar aren't dangerous; he has asked them to believe that he is bigger! God is faithful and strong enough to keep them safe and do exactly as he said he would.

Sister, we live in a world that is scary. Sex trafficking is real. Murders are reported every day. Christians are being targeted and maligned. And yet, our God is bigger!

What person or situation is making you feel like a grasshopper?

....

....

....

....

Think of that situation from God's perspective. How have you made people big and God small?

....

....

....

....

....

How has your fear caused you to forget God?

....

....

....

Sarah's Fearlessness

Any cause for fear is an occasion for faith. If anyone had cause for fear in this story, it's Sarah. She was in a terribly vulnerable position, all because her husband chose to lie. And yet, I wonder if this was one of the situations Peter had in mind when he wrote about Sarah in his letter.

Read 1 Peter 3:1-7.

What is the "even if" situation that Peter mentions in verse 1? How does this apply to Sarah's situation in Genesis 20?

....

....

....

According to verses 1-2, what is a wife's most effective way of persuading her husband to obey God?

....

....

....

Sarah was beautiful in the eyes of men. What makes a woman beautiful in the eyes of God (vv. 3-4)?

....

....

....

....

How can we learn to adorn ourselves and become like Sarah (vv. 5–6)?

....

....

....

....

When I hear that we should follow Sarah's example of being fearless, I want to turn in my Bible and read the story, don't you? I wonder if we just have. Peter doesn't say which part of Sarah's story he's referring to when he calls her fearless, but there isn't any part more likely than this.

Sarah is silent in our Genesis 20 text, but as we look at her overall story, this is a turning point. In the next scene, we're going to see her living by faith, so it stands to reason that this is the place when Sarah decided to rehearse what God said, remember what he had done, and not to fear "anything that is frightening" (1 Peter 3:6)—including being taken by another king. There in Abimelech's harem, Sarah was completely vulnerable and had plenty to fear, but perhaps she settled herself with God's promises. She certainly could have!

So how do we not fear any frightening thing? We remember just how big our God is—so big, he towers over the world and makes it his footstool (Isaiah 66:1). Only when you remember just how big and strong God is do you see the threats of this world in their proper proportion.

God's Grace in Gerar

Our friend George is wise, kind, generous, and fun. He causes every group to gel and makes every gathering more fun. But George's middle school–aged daughter seems not to have inherited his charms. She is consistently rude, demanding, and sassy. If George is sunshine on your back, this girl is sleet in your face. And yet George treats her like a princess. One day George was building a bonfire for a group of us, and his daughter interrupted to ask him to do something for her. When he didn't immediately respond, she stomped into the middle of the group of adults and loudly demanded he help her immediately.

George calmly led his daughter to the shadows where he could gently correct her in private. After she went huffing into the house, someone gave George an opportunity to complain about parenting teens, but he valiantly defended his daughter's honor. "It's hard to be a teen these days," he said softly. "She's a good kid. I love her."

George's endless grace both baffled me and caused my opinion of him to soar higher yet.

Grace is like that. In Gerar, God put his power on display, but it's his display of grace that makes our hearts soar.

The Grieving Women of Gerar

Let's set the backdrop. Something horrible has been happening in Gerar, and it started after the king's newly acquired bride, Sarah, moved into the harem.

Read Genesis 20:1-18.

What tragic circumstances have the women in Abimelech's household been experiencing, and what is causing this?

....

....

At least how long has this been going on? (Think about menstruation.)

....

How did Sarah describe the cause of her hardship in Genesis 16:2?

....

....

....

There have probably been miscarriages in Gerar. Certainly, no new pregnancies. And there in Abimelech's harem, Sarah had a front-row seat to the tears and pain. In a culture that so elevated bearing children, this was devastating.

You and I will need to set aside our thoughts on harems and polygamy for a moment so we can consider the grief and sorrow this represents—a grief that Sarah was well acquainted with. God had closed all of their wombs, just like he closed hers.

Sarah's Secret

Like I said in lesson 3, I believe that during these weeks and months in Abimelech's harem, Sarah's faith was coming alive. Perhaps she was doing the math and recognizing that if God promised she would have a child nine or ten months from now (Genesis 18:10), Sarah needed to get home to her husband. There was nothing she could do about this, of course, but it looked as if God already had.

God is sovereign over details that no one else is aware of (like a woman's period) and details that people cannot ultimately engineer (like human reproduction). As the women of Abimelech's household began to be affected by a strange, womb-closing outbreak, Sarah was likely watching from the shadows, wondering, "Is this what I think it is?" It's not something you'd want to take credit for.

She'd been there long enough for there to be disruptions in the women's cycles, but apparently not long enough for Abimelech to trace the infertility issues (and Genesis 20:6 and 17 might also imply impotence) back to her. God was the one who revealed her secret.

Reread Genesis 20:3–10, recognizing that all of Abimelech's household is grieving over infertility.

What is Abimelech guilty of, according to God?

....

....

What do we learn about Abimelech's character as he confronts Abraham? What words or phrases give the impression of his concern and sense of responsibility for his people?

....

....

....

Abimelech is torn up. His women are grieving, and he is at fault. He didn't know he had taken a married woman, yet he's being held accountable. He's willing to do whatever it takes to make things right with this God he had offended—and this other man's wife.

Exonerating Sarah

Now that we have our backdrop in place, let's shine the spotlight on Sarah. As we've traveled with her, we have watched her carry the shame of being the "brittle branch" for decades. She has also endured the pain of being looked down upon by her servant, then brushed aside by her husband's passivity. In addition, we've learned that in every new town, she's been asked to assume the risk (for her husband's safety) of calling herself his sister.

This woman has endured a lot of dishonor. And yet, by God's grace, she's about to be exonerated by the most unlikely source: a pagan king.

Read Genesis 20:14–18.

What does Abimelech give Abraham? Which gift is on behalf of Sarah?

....

....

Does Abimelech give his gifts before or after learning Sarah was the cause of suffering?

....

....

What does he say to Sarah about the purpose of the silver? Why will this be important in the near future?

....

....

....

What did Abimelech say about Abraham and Sarah living in his land?

....

....

....

If you recall, back in Egypt (Genesis 12:16–20), Pharaoh gave gifts as a bride price, but then when he learned Sarah was the cause of the plagues, he addressed Abraham (not her), and kicked them both out of Egypt for good. This experience is entirely different.

First, a thousand pieces of silver was nothing to sneeze at. The highest price you could pay for one bride was fifty pieces of silver,[4] so Abimelech's gift is the equivalent of twenty brides. And this bride was going back to her rightful husband.

When Abimelech says, "This is to cover the offense" (Genesis 20:16 NIV), the Hebrew literally means, "to cover the eyes." It means that Abimelech is closing the blinds on anything that might cause others to look down on Sarah.[5]

Abimelech is not only inviting Abraham and his "sister" to stay in Gerar, he's painting them as honored guests—not the town villains, who have caused all the infertility. Abimelech has spent a small fortune declaring two things: Sarah had a valid complaint against him (she was married), and he is cleared of culpability (he didn't sleep with her).

This is amazing! Look how God is protecting Sarah's honor. Now, when Sarah has a baby in the coming year, there will be no shadow of a doubt about who the father is, since Abimelech has just made a public announcement that he didn't touch her. What an amazing turn of events in just twenty-four hours! God truly does work all things together for good, for those who are called according to his purpose (Romans 8:28).

How has God sovereignly arranged for Sarah to be honored and vindicated?

....

....

....

....

....

....

Recall a time you've been dishonored, publicly or in the eyes of an individual. Share any ways God has used this for good.

....

....

....

....

Flawed Abraham

The story doesn't end with the silver changing hands. God has one more thing to show us about himself, and this time, he'll use Abraham. Compare Abraham and Abimelech so far in this story and check all that apply:

ABRAHAM	ABIMELECH	
		...is morally earnest and wants to do what's right.
		...is willing to make up excuses to prove his innocence.
		...is selfish and not thinking of how his actions impact others.
		...is deeply concerned about Sarah's honor.
		...is wise and willing to overlook offenses.
		...has responded to evil with good.
		...has responded to good with evil.

Read Genesis 20:7.

God says, "Return [Abraham's] wife, for he is a

_____."

What must Abraham do for all to be healed?

....

....

....

....

How is God once again keeping his promise from back in Genesis 12:3?

....

....

....

....

If you look at who wronged who, it should be Abraham giving gifts, not Abimelech. The curse on Gerar was because of his lie. And now our cowardly swindler is being honored as "prophet."

Um . . . what? I could imagine calling Abraham a prophet back when he was pleading with God to spare Sodom. He seemed honorable then, but not here in Gerar.

Theology 2.0

Abraham has done what "should never be done" (Genesis 20:9 CSB). He has lied, put Sarah at risk, and exposed a whole bunch of people to a curse—and it's through him that all the peoples of the earth are to be *blessed* (Genesis 12:3). Again, the Bible isn't a story about people getting what they deserve from God; it's a story about them getting what they *don't* deserve. And this story tacks on, "Even people who know better."

Have you ever watched somebody who knew better plummet to faith's basement? Maybe a wife who used to lead Bible study has left her husband. Or a pastor who preached against adultery is addicted to pornography. Perhaps your child who once earnestly memorized Bible verses has forsaken God for the world. Or maybe you're the one who has done things that dishonor God even when you knew better. Maybe you do these things still.

Sister, God always keeps his promises—not because we're always faithful, but because he is. And when God is faithful to somebody who knows better, it puts a spotlight on his grace.

Consider what we learn about God in this story. For each pair, checkmark the one that rings true:

__ God is fiercely protective of his own.
__ God is fiercely protective of whoever is more righteous.

__ God demands that his chosen ones never fail.
__ God never fails his chosen ones.

__ God uses perfect people to represent himself to the world.
__ God uses flawed people to represent himself to the world.

__ God wants his chosen ones to pray for the hurting and broken.
__ God wants his chosen ones to solve the problems of the hurting and broken.

__ God is most interested in showcasing our honor and wisdom to the world.
__ God is most interested in showcasing his own honor and wisdom to the world.

A Showcase of Grace

Perhaps the place we see God's grace most clearly in this story is at the end, when, instead of quashing Abraham, God calls upon him for honorable service.

In Genesis 20:17:

Who prayed and what was the effect?

....

....

....

....

How was God's power displayed?

....

....

....

....

How was God's grace displayed?

....

....

....

....

Abraham prayed, and healing spread. The people of Gerar learned of God's power, both through their suffering and through God stopping it. But in Abraham's flaws, they also got to see glimpses of God's grace.

Remember our friend George, whose endless grace toward his daughter baffled me? If George's daughter was just as charming as him, I might not have had occasion to wonder at George's patient, godly character. Like that, Abraham's big flaws highlight God's big, amazing grace.

This story of Abraham falling so quickly from faith makes no sense. But the big storyline of the Bible makes no sense if you edit out God's grace. If the story was meant to reveal God's righteousness (but not grace), at the apex of the story—Jesus's death and resurrection—we would see God rescuing his righteous son from the cross and destroying all the sinners who put him there. From start to finish, the Bible is a story that displays God's grace.

By his grace, God chooses undeserving sinners.

By his grace, God shows his faithfulness to the faithless.

By his grace, God uses flawed servants like Abraham to bless the nations.

By his grace, God uses flawed servants like us to spread his story to the world.

Considering Him Faithful

Sarah lived through the repeat of a horrible situation. Abraham lied again, and she was taken to yet another king's harem, where another household was cursed with infertility because of her. But God flashed his power, and Sarah was exonerated and returned to her husband—just in time.

RETELL

Summarize the story of Abraham and Sarah in Gerar, using these quotes to guide you:

"She is my sister." (Genesis 20:2)

"You are a dead man." (Genesis 20:3)

"What did you see?" (Genesis 20:10)

"There is absolutely no fear of God in this place." (Genesis 20:11 CSB)

"I have given your brother a thousand pieces of silver." (Genesis 20:16)

....

....

....

....

....

....

....

....

....

....

REFLECT

Review some key points from the week and reflect on how God is inviting you to respond.

By taking Sarah, Abimelech has interfered with God's promises about the coming year, and tangled himself in something more colossal than he realizes. Yet because of God, Abimelech never touched Sarah.

How does it impact you to know that God's plan for your salvation (which involved Sarah having a baby) was kept safe by him?

....

....

....

....

If you are in Christ, from an eternal perspective, nothing can touch you. How does this help you face a particularly frightening situation in your life?

....

....

....

....

Abraham said there was no fear of God in Gerar, yet ironically, Abimelech had more fear of God than Abraham did. As Abraham's fear of people got big, his fear of God shrunk.

Do you have a big view of God? How does your right fear of God help you to "not fear anything that is frightening" (1 Peter 3:6)?

....

....

....

....

What sinful behaviors (like Abraham's lying) reveal your shrunken view of God? How does this story give you a correct, big view of God?

....

....

....

....

Choose a fear that you often struggle with and play "Three Truths and a Fear." Select truths about God or promises he has made.

Truth: ....

Truth: ....

Truth: ....

Fear: ....

Ninety-nine-year-old Abraham was cowardly and self-serving, even though he knew better. Yet God kept his promises anyway—which put a spotlight on God's grace. God doesn't keep his promises because of our faithfulness, but because of his.

How have you tarnished your testimony? How will you allow this situation to showcase God's grace?

....

....

....

....

How are you being affected by some other person whose faith is plummeting? What are you learning about God's faithfulness?

....

....

....

....

....

....

REHEARSE

In this part of the story, God uses infertility (and potentially impotence) to put protection around Sarah's womb. This is not just a story about Sarah having a baby, it's a story about preserving our salvation, which will come through Sarah's offspring, Jesus. God shows that he will stop at nothing to keep his promise to save us.

How is God's faithfulness to his promises revealed in this part of Sarah's story?

....

....

....

....

Will you be shaped by God's promises? Choose a meaningful promise from appendix 2 (page 291) along with a verse to memorize. Write them both below.

....

....

....

....

....

....

....

....

....

....

....

....

....

....

Laughter
and
Perspective

Laughter and Perspective

Faith's Tipping Point

We're here! We've finally arrived at the place on Sarah's timeline where God closes a whole bunch of parentheses. It has been an arduous journey of disappointments, doubts, and testing. But after a much longer stretch than Sarah ever anticipated, God is ready to do for her as he promised. And yet, there's one more important tipping point in Sarah's story, which has so much to teach us about our own faith.

Read Genesis 21:1–2.

What three phrases in these verses emphasize that God is keeping his promises?

....

....

....

....

What time is verse 2 referring to? (See Genesis 18:10.)

....

....

How are the promises fulfilled for Sarah?

....

....

What does this story teach us about God's character?

....

....

....

Active Faith

I pointed out earlier that Hebrews 11 lists not what people believed by faith, but what they *did* by faith. Moses split the Red Sea. Daniel braved the lions. Rahab hid the spies. These people did radical things because they believed radical promises. Their stories make me want to get up on my chair and cheer—then step down and live my own radical, shaped-by-the-promise life.

But when I get to Sarah's verse in Hebrews 11, I feel a little silly standing on my chair.

Write Hebrews 11:11 and circle the first two (ESV) or three (NIV) words:

....

....

....

....

For a long time, I was baffled at Sarah being included here. Her story was so unlike the others. Of course, every baby is a miracle, but I speak on some authority when I say that expectant moms do nothing to knit their babies together. They simply eat and sleep and watch their bellies grow. The new little human coming into existence is all God's doing—and this was doubly true of Sarah, who was "past the age." This miracle happened *to* Sarah. Compared to the other stories of radical faith, I wasn't sure she had demonstrated the type of stand-on-your-chair faith worthy of Hebrews 11.

But then one day it dawned on me that there was something that Sarah had to *do* in order to have this baby. And that "something" required radical faith.

The Appointed Time

Draw a timeline of the past year in Sarah's life, using what you've learned from Genesis 18, 19, 20, and 21:1:

How does knowing the timing of Sarah's pregnancy in Genesis 21:1 shed new light on the details disclosed in these quotes from the previous chapter?

"Therefore I have not let you touch her." (Genesis 20:6 csb)

....

....

....

"It is a verification of your honor." (Genesis 20:16 csb)

....

....

....

Abimelech's household was affected by infertility (Genesis 20:18), which is marked by months, not days or weeks. Using your timeline above, how many months do you think Sarah has been in Gerar?

In Genesis 20:14, what happened to Sarah? Considering your timeline, what must Sarah do shortly after this for God's promise to be kept at the "appointed time" (Genesis 21:2)?

What detail of Sarah's sex life was disclosed in her self-talk back in Genesis 18:12? How does this emphasize Sarah's faith?

How many years have gone by since God first promised to make of Abraham a great nation? Look at your timeline on page 17. How does this detail emphasize Sarah's faith?

What detail about Sarah's cycle is revealed in Genesis 18:11? How does this detail emphasize Sarah's faith?

Sarah's Great Faith

For twenty-four years, Sarah has been the brittle branch on the family tree. She had endured decades of infertility and is now in menopause. And now, can you imagine Sarah—at age eighty-nine—saying to Abraham, "Want to try for a baby tonight?"

Oh, sister. This required great faith. The active kind.

In my book, *Control Girl*, I said that Sarah hoping for a child was as preposterous as me—now at age fifty-two, after a lifetime of being unable to do a back handspring—hoping to become an Olympic gymnast. "That window of opportunity has been closed. Painted shut. Boarded over," I wrote. "Imagine how foolish I would look, showing up in my leotard at the US Olympic trials."[1]

I hope that mental image makes you laugh. Here's what made Sarah laugh: the idea of her sleeping with her husband after all this time. The window of opportunity to conceive a child had been closed. Any hope of a baby had been boarded shut—and along with it, the intimacy in Sarah's marriage. And yet God was asking Sarah to pry open her heart and her body in hopes of conceiving a child. Can you even imagine how hard it was for Sarah to be vulnerable enough to hope?

So in the end, I take back my critique of Sarah's inclusion in Hebrews 11. She exercised radical faith when she slipped into bed with her husband, expecting the miraculous.

By Faith

Let's take a closer look at this verse that our study has been anchored in.

Read Hebrews 11:11 out loud.

Look carefully and circle the correct verb (check the ESV or CSB):

> **By faith Sarah . . .**
>
> > **conceived offspring.**
> >
> > **received power to conceive.**

This is the only time that Hebrews 11 mentions someone being given power. What do you think sets Sarah apart from the others?

....

....

....

When have you seen God supply the supernatural power to do something "impossible"—such as loving someone who was difficult, giving generously, or grieving with hope? How did this require faith?

....

....

....

....

....

All Things Considered

All of the other people mentioned in Hebrews 11 did big, extraordinary things. But Sarah did something she had done many times over the years: she slept with her husband. Yet this time, she conceived a baby. Why this time? What changed? Well, we know that God time-stamped his promise, but the verse gives us one more explanation.

In Hebrews 11:11, find the connector word "because" or "since," which signals an explanation coming. What is the explanation for Sarah's power? (Look at what comes after the connector.)

....

....

....

....

Remember that the word "consider" is an accounting word. It's like a banker who considers you for a loan, then stacks up the evidence to decide if you're trustworthy. That's what Sarah is doing. She's considering the evidence she has about God. She's stacking it up. And what specifically is she considering about God?

"She considered him _____ who had _____."
(Hebrews 11:11)

Sarah looks back over her shoulder at the past twenty-some years, asking, "Is God good for his word? Has he kept his promises? Has he been faithful?" Perhaps she thinks back to the day they arrived after walking a thousand miles, and God appeared and showed her husband the land. Or maybe she recounts the way God cursed both Pharaoh's and Abimelech's households with plagues, on her behalf. Perhaps she recalls the mysterious visitors who came to lunch, restating the promise of a son in her presence. Would this be enough to tip your scale?

Whatever data Sarah "considered" as she collected and stacked up evidence, she found enough to create a tipping point for her faith—and this is what activated God's power.

Now, God's power is not dependent on our faith. He is free to do whatever wonderful thing he wants to, and will not be held hostage by us. But often times he does wait for our faith before he unleashes his power. Imagine if God hadn't required Sarah's "active faith" and she just woke up pregnant at age eighty-nine. God could have done this, of course. But like we've said from the beginning, God wants for us to be shaped by his promises. He often allows us to experience impossible situations that stretch and grow our faith.

Is that not what we're seeing in Sarah? Just a couple of chapters back, she was scoffing at the idea of sleeping with her husband. But now she has the radical belief that God is going to give her a baby. If your eighty-nine-year-old mom or grandma said this, you'd be concerned about her mind—and the idea of Sarah's pregnancy is no less absurd. Yet with her logic and wisdom, Sarah has concluded that if God promised, it will happen. So by faith, she sleeps with her husband.

God loves it when we consider him faithful.

Faith's Tipping Point

If you think of faith like a teeter-totter, "considering" is what causes the shift from doubt to faith. When you live in doubt, it's because you've considered and stacked up all of the reasons why a particular thing is impossible. When you live by faith, it's because you've considered and stacked up all of God's promises and his perfect track record of faithfulness.

Fill in some of Sarah's doubts about having a baby, such as infertility.

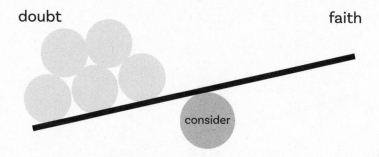

Now, faith doesn't ignore all of the doubts; it just considers or gives more weight to God's power, and asks, "Is anything too wonderful for God?"

Fill in some examples of God keeping his promises that Sarah might have considered as she looked back over the past twenty-four years.

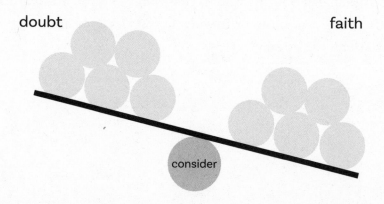

In what situation do you most need God's supernatural power? Is your marriage hanging by a thread? Has your prodigal child been wandering for decades? Have you received a grim diagnosis? Summarize the situation, then fill the diagram below with all the factors there are to consider in your situation.

Stack up your reasons to doubt God, your fear of the future, and your "what ifs." Then on the other side, stack up your evidence about God. Include stories of his faithfulness, either in the Bible or your life. Add any of his promises that come to mind.

Use this exercise to consider him faithful who has promised.

Situation where I need God's supernatural power:_____

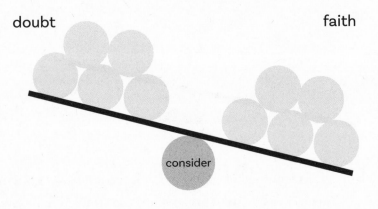

The *tipping point* is when your faith activates because you've given weight to God's promises and character. For Sarah, it was sleeping with her husband. For you it might be forgiving someone, trusting God enough to give generously, or grieving the loss of a loved one with hope that you'll see them again.

How is God asking you to actively live by faith and be shaped by his promise? Record your response as your "tipping point."

....

....

....

....

....

....

....

Her Promised Son

The moment Sarah conceived Isaac was an incredible tipping point of her faith. God took notice of Sarah and did for her what he promised (Genesis 21:1). He unleashed supernatural power in her life. As Sarah's arms closed around her miraculous baby son, God's parentheses closed on his promises to her and to us.

Laughter Is Born

Every good story is built around a character who wants something. Often she faces a challenge or an obstacle to her goal, and the tension is resolved when the character overcomes. This is that moment in Sarah's story. She finally has the baby she's longed for.

But more than just a story about having a baby, Sarah's story is inextricably tied to the bigger, overarching story of the Bible and its main character, God. So what does *God* want? That's an interesting question because God lacks nothing and has never met a foe he couldn't immediately annihilate, nor does God's character change or develop. Not much of a story, right? And yet, God—in his glorious, selfless humility—adopts our plight as his own. Ultimately, he sends his son to enter our story as the conquering hero who restores the community, peace, flourishing, and belonging encapsulated in that Eden word, *shalom*.

But in these early chapters, as God kicks off his re-Edenizing plan, he selects a new line of people (the Abrahams) who will live in a new place (Canaan). Ten seconds in, we get bad news. These new characters are no better than the first. How will God develop and reshape Abraham and Sarah into Eden-like people? He will use the chiseling effect of his promises.

Now here's where it really gets interesting. At first, it seems as though what God wants and what Sarah wants is the same: he promises children to her husband. She is elated! Then gradually, she is deflated. We feel for her. As the months roll by and the pages turn, we wonder, "Why, God?

Why not give her this child you've promised?"

Yet God is using his promises to develop Sarah and reshape her into someone new. He uses the long arm of time to tip her chin so that she'll search his face. He uses the disparity between his promise and her reality to invite her to "consider him faithful who had promised." And when she does, she is transformed! We hear it best in her laughter.

A Transforming God

Read Genesis 21:1–7.

How old is Sarah when she gives birth? How much time has passed since God first implied Abraham would have a child? Check your timeline on page 17.

What can we learn about God's timing from Sarah's timeline?

"Isaac" means laughter. Why is this a fitting name? (Think of Genesis 17:17 and 18:12–13.)

Draw a line from Sarah's quotes (Genesis 18:12, 15; 21:6, 7 NIV) to each sentiment or tone you hear in her words:

"After I am worn out and my lord is old, will I now have this pleasure?"

"I did not laugh."

"God has brought me laughter."

"Everyone who hears about this will laugh with me."

"Who would have said to Abraham that Sarah would nurse children?"

Delight

Cynicism

Amazement

Defensiveness

Doubt

Joy

Skepticism

Embarrassment

Wonder

Happiness

What change or progression do you hear in Sarah's laughter in Genesis 21:6–7?

....

....

....

Read Psalm 30:11–12. How does this encapsulate Sarah's experience?

....

....

....

....

....

Holding Laughter

Before Sarah was showing, I suspect she only told Abraham that she was pregnant. Can you imagine? People would have thought she'd lost her mind. And doubly so, if she said this pregnancy was "planned."

Even back when they first left Haran, this idea was preposterous. It was likely a secret they had kept from the beginning. People probably found it baffling (and maybe amusing) when ninety-nine-year-old Abram changed his name to "exalted father." And Sarah's humiliation about having no child had weighed on her for decades. The very topic of her childlessness (let alone God's promise) was so fraught with emotion, it probably wasn't something you brought up in casual conversation around the camp.

Remember that at this point, Abraham is a very wealthy, powerful man. Back in Genesis 14:14, we learned that he had 318 trained men born into his household. Surely, that number has grown. By now, his camp probably numbered in the thousands.

Abraham was a chieftain. You might think of him as a sheik. He was a decorated war hero (Genesis 14:17). And Sarah, his queen, was *pregnant*? Oh, this news would have traveled fast no matter how old she was! But to be expecting her first child on her ninetieth birthday was simply astonishing. When this news broke, I doubt anyone talked about anything else!

And then, Isaac was born. Can you just picture the joy and laughter as Abraham carried his armful of "laughter" around for all to see?

Laugh with Me

Genesis 21:6–7 gives us a quote from Sarah after Isaac is born. Twice she mentions other people and their reactions. What is Sarah imagining people have or will say?

Verse 6: ....
....

Verse 7: ....
....

What extra phrase in verse 3 offers emphasis, and why? (Remember there are two sons.)

....
....
....

What suffering was Sarah referring to in Genesis 16:5? How has Sarah been set free from the concern over being laughed at? Note Genesis 21:6 in your answer.

....
....
....
....

Count the number of times Abraham is mentioned (including pronouns) in Genesis 21:1–7. How does this contrast with Genesis 16:1?

....
....
....

In God's story, how does this baby remind you of Jesus?

....
....
....
....

How is Sarah experiencing a moment full of shalom? Imagine your own personal moment of shalom, when something you've longed for is satisfied. Describe what you might see, hear, and feel.

....

....

....

....

The Fulfillment of Laughter

This baby is a big deal because Abraham is a big deal—in both Sarah's story and God's. As Sarah presents her warlord, chieftain husband with a new baby boy, her honor is restored and God's honor is celebrated. He has done what he promised! He has proven himself faithful. And Sarah is changed.

Not too long ago, Sarah was crushed under the weight of being laughed at by the watching world. Yet God has turned her insecurity, envy, and sorrow into lighthearted rejoicing—and now Sarah is inviting others to laugh with her over what only God could have done. It's just a taste of what's to come for those who belong to God.

I called my friend Renell a couple of months ago, excited to give her an update on a situation that she has been praying with me about for a long time. I said, "It almost sounds like God is giving me everything I've been pleading for. I know that's unlikely. It probably won't happen." She said, "But Shan, it could! Maybe God is doing something amazing!"

I called her this week to say, "I think God *is* doing something amazing!" and we laughed together in awe. Sometimes it feels risky to hope because we don't want to be disappointed. We keep our hopes private, or only share them with a close friend. We believe God *can*, but we're not sure if he *will*. Yet when he *does*, we throw open the doors to our private world and invite everyone to laugh with us!

When you described a room full of shalom, did you include laughter? I love that God names Isaac "laughter," because it sets the tone for the rest of his plan. Really, it's the plan to save us! He wants to eventually give us everything that we—as the human race—have lost. He's preparing a place filled with shalom, where we will laugh together in amazement over all he has done.

Has God filled your life with new laughter by giving you something you longed for? Describe it.

....

....

....

....

....

What are you still pleading with God for? How is God using the chiseling effect of his promises to change you?

....

....

....

What is your ultimate promise in Revelation 21:3–4?

....

....

....

What does 2 Peter 3:8–10 say about God's timing?

....

....

....

A Resurrection Sunday

It had been a year since Jill learned about her husband Mark's affair, and he wasn't softening. Jill's friends were telling her it was probably time to start planning for a different outcome than she was hoping for. Then one morning, Mark came to Jill with a piece of paper in his hand that he'd been carrying around, which listed all of the things wrong with her and with their marriage. He said, "I'm filing for a divorce."

Jill was stunned. She prayed silently, *Lord, what should I even say?* What came out of her mouth was, "Mark, Jesus didn't want to go to the cross. In the garden of Gethsemane, he had to do battle in order to surrender himself and pray, 'Not my will but yours be done'" (Luke 22:42).

Mark said, "Wait. Is today Easter?" She told him it was. Mark said, "I think I'm going to pray that prayer."

Jill was astonished. Mark was going to pray that *God's* will be done? She wasn't sure what, but something was happening. Even Mark's physical demeanor began to change as he prayed. Mark has since told her that in that moment, he sensed God saying, "If you'll give me that list, I'll take care of the rest." Mark was craving the peace that is only ours when we surrender control to God. And so, three minutes after declaring he was divorcing Jill, he looked up from his prayer of surrender and said, "Can we go to church?" That

Listen to more of Jill Savage's story on Shannon's Live Like It's True podcast. Go to shannonpopkin.com /promises.

Easter Sunday morning, God was resurrecting a marriage that didn't even have a pulse.

This story raises the question, "Is anything too wonderful for God?" I opened Instagram last week and saw Mark and Jill with their faces turned toward each other, laughing. They were sharing about their new marriage curriculum—which they would be the first to tell you is laughable, considering all they've been through. Sister, our God can do *anything*.

WEEK 6

A Split in the Family Tree

Isaac is a big boy now (probably about age three), and Abraham holds a party to celebrate. Can you imagine little Isaac running around in his miniature sandals, his dark curls tousled by the breeze? I picture the women trying to tickle him as he giggles, and the men tossing him up in the air.

But the laughter stops and the party comes to an awkward halt when somebody laughs *at* this little boy named "Laughter."

Read Genesis 21:8–11.

How has laughter created conflict in the story (v. 9), and why is this ironic?

....

....

....

Check your timeline on page 17. If Isaac is three, how old is Ishmael?

....

Why might Ishmael feel animosity toward Isaac?

....

....

....

Why might Sarah feel animosity toward Ishmael?

....

....

....

Does Sarah's demand in verse 10 seem appropriate to you? Why or why not?

....

....

....

In Genesis 21:1–21, how many times is Ishmael's name used? What does this foreshadow?

....

....

....

Party's Over

We notice how the author of Genesis begins to sunset Ishmael by no longer using his name, but Ishmael feels the exclusion in real time.

Little Isaac must have been the bane of Ishmael's existence. Every time Ishmael turned around, there was his father doting on his new son, born to his old wife. There had always been tension between Ishmael's mom (Hagar) and his dad's first wife (Sarah), but when Isaac was born, the family dynamic became combustible. Then, at the party, Sarah lit a match.

I empathize with Ishmael, but that doesn't make his behavior right. One commentator suggests Ishmael's mocking involved playing "heir Isaac."[2] But Sarah's behavior isn't right either. It only takes one glance at this son of the "other woman" mocking her son for Sarah to boil over in rage.

If you've experienced broken family relationships, this story doesn't surprise you. You know how deep emotions can run, and how many "sides" there are to every story. But here's what I think *will* surprise you: God's response.

Read Genesis 21:10-13.

How does Abraham feel about Sarah's demand, and why (v. 11)?

....

....

How does God tell Abraham to respond to Sarah's demand, and why (v. 12)?

....

....

What assurance does God give Abraham about Ishmael (v. 13)?

....

....

What reason does Sarah give for her demand in Genesis 21:10? How does this align with what God said to Abraham back in Genesis 17:18-19?

....

....

....

How would the Wildernites (who now saw Ishmael's descendants as a threat) have interpreted this story?

....

....

....

Choosing the Younger Son

In a patriarchal society, the oldest son always got the lion's share of the inheritance. To flip that order would be like me saying you should pay for *my* son's college expenses rather than paying for *your* son's college expenses. It was just wildly backward. Abraham's wealth also added to the tension. The dude was so rich, college tuition would've been like pocket change. So, back when God gave Abraham the news that Ishmael wouldn't be his heir and Isaac would (Genesis 17:18–19), it was utterly shocking.

Abraham knew that all of his wealth and someday-land was from God. It makes sense that God could flip the inheritance rules and divvy things up however he liked. But that didn't make it easy. Abraham had been mulling over the challenge of how to implement this, literally for *years*. Like any father, Abraham loved both of his boys and wanted them to grow up together. But God was telling him to listen to Sarah and send his firstborn son away.

Read Genesis 21:14.

What does Abraham send Hagar and Ishmael off with?

....

....

How is Abraham's response that of an obedient steward, not an owner?

....

....

Circle any examples you're familiar with of God choosing the younger or unexpected son:

David	Saul	Daniel
Esau	Jacob	Jesus

Sarah's Demand

At first glance, it looks like Sarah—whose reaction seems disproportionately harsh—is having a "Control Girl moment." Did she even get up early to watch Hagar and Ishmael disappear into the morning mist? Did she mutter "good riddance" as she walked by their empty tent?

Only Abraham is mentioned at the send-off (Genesis 21:14), and he doesn't even spare a donkey or an armed man. Instead, he loads the bread and water onto *Hagar's* shoulders. What a lot for her to carry (and not just physically). The most shocking part is that God endorses Sarah's spiteful demands.

Why, God? I wonder. *This seems so unlike you.* But then, the next part of the story actually *is* quite like God. I wish we had time to study it more carefully, but in short: when Ishmael is about to die of thirst, God hears his parched cry* and opens Hagar's eyes to a nearby well. Ishmael lives and becomes not just a free man, but a king who raises twelve princes. (See Genesis 21:17–21 and 25:16.) So, while God only establishes his covenant with Isaac, God still blesses Abraham's firstborn, Ishmael.

For now, let's turn our attention back to the camp, where Sarah has gone ballistic and we have to assume that when Abraham sends his firstborn son and second wife away with only a day's provisions, he's doing "whatever Sarah says" (Genesis 21:12). This makes me shake my head and say,

*This is particularly tender, because though Hagar was the one crying out, God hears Ishmael—meaning he must be leaning very near to this boy who's dying of thirst. It was God who gave Ishmael his name, which means, "God hears." See Genesis 16:11.

"Sarah, Sarah . . . where is that beautiful faith we saw in you just a few verses back?"

Yet the longer I study Sarah's "mama bear" moment, the more I actually *do* see trace evidences of her faith—even though her execution was lacking. Let's look at some of the reasons we can conclude that Sarah is being shaped by God's promises.

Look again at the reason Sarah gives for her drastic demands:

> For the son of this slave woman shall not be heir with my son Isaac. (Genesis 21:10)

What is Sarah adamant about Ishmael not being? Circle the word.

How does this align with what God said in Genesis 17:20–21?

....

....

....

....

Notice God's reason for telling Abraham to listen to Sarah in Genesis 21:12 (csb):

> **"Because your offspring will be traced through Isaac."**
>
> **What does God say will happen through Isaac? Circle the phrase.**

Why do you think Ishmael needed to be sent away for this to happen?

....

....

....

....

Fiery Faith

Back when my friend Chey was taking an adoption class, she was taught to make and quickly keep promises to her son so he would learn to trust her. For instance, she would say, "I promise we'll go to the park today." And then, they would go to the park. Or, "I'll take you to the zoo on Saturday." Then she would take him to the zoo on Saturday. This method of building trust by keeping the parentheses in tight makes sense to us, right?

Now suppose on the day Chey promised her son ice cream after school, she hears from the school principal that her son has been sent to the office for hitting a friend on the playground. *Oh great*, Chey thinks. But when she picks him up, her son explains: "That boy was saying you aren't going to buy me ice cream. But I said you are!" Then he looks into her eyes and asks, "Are you?"

Chey wouldn't be pleased about the hitting, but she would be pleased that apparently her son is learning to trust her, right? So much so, he's willing to defend her promise as true. I think this is what is happening with Sarah. You see, Sarah believes that Isaac's descendants (offspring) will inherit the land that they are standing on. And yet in a moment of clarity, her eyes widen to what has always been true: Ishmael is a threat to Isaac's inheritance.

After witnessing Ishmael's mocking, Sarah sees where this is all headed. This jealous rivalry wasn't something Ishmael was simply going to grow out of. His domineering contentiousness had been prophesied by the Lord before he was even born (Genesis 16:12). Plus, Ishmael would always be older. Isaac would always be vulnerable to bullying. And Sarah would not always be around to step in. So she's stepping in while she still can and demanding something drastic: a split to the family tree.

The idea that two brothers *not* be coheirs was so unconventional, it's not something Sarah would have thought of on her own. As Sarah not just suggests but demands that Ishmael be sent away, we see something that was missing before. Sarah is being shaped by God's promises. She not only believes them, she's willing to defend the promise as true. For God had said, "As for Ishmael . . . I will certainly bless him . . . but I will confirm my covenant with Isaac" (Genesis 17:20–21 CSB).

Do you see what has happened in our girl, Sarah? Gone is the doubt! In its place is a fiery faith! Ishmael was Sarah's idea in the first place, but that was back when she lacked faith that God would fulfill his promise. Now it's Sarah's idea to send Ishmael away because she's filled with faith that God will fulfill his promise.

What evidences of active faith do you see in Sarah's reaction?

....

....

....

....

How is Sarah's reaction proportionate to the value she put on this inheritance?

....

....

....

....

Putting a Price Tag on Our Inheritance

Nobody sues over an inheritance worth a dollar. But when two parties believe an inheritance will be worth millions, they're far more invested in what they stand to gain. For the Abrahams, the biggest part of the inheritance they're passing down is something they don't own yet. They were still living in tents, remember? Canaan doesn't yet belong to them, but God has said it will. So Sarah's reaction was commensurate with her faith. And there's a sense in which this is true for you and me, as well.

Sister, you and I haven't been promised land, wealth, or a nation-sized family—at least not in the here and now. But if we are "in Christ," then we too have an inheritance coming: we are the coheirs of God's promises, passed down from Abraham. We are the people God is restoring to his presence, who will one day live with him in that shalom-filled place.

Have you thought recently about how much this inheritance is worth? Have you considered how important it is to let the generation following you know how much this inheritance is worth? If it was only worth a dollar, you might shrug off letting them know. But sister, the inheritance that God is keeping for us is worth far more than millions. What price tag can we put on being reconciled to God, forgiven of our sin debt, and coheirs of heaven, filled with pleasures forevermore? I don't want my kids—or anyone else I have influence over—to miss out on this. Do you?

Now, it would be a mistake to emulate Sarah with her white knuckles and harsh demands. But on the other hand, it would also be a mistake to passively do nothing about the encroaching threats to our own faith or the faith of the next generation.

Assessing the Threats

How are we like Isaac, according to Galatians 3:29?

....

....

....

....

What does 1 Peter 1:3–5 say about your inheritance?

....

....

....

Considering the great worth of your inheritance, look around and
do a quick threat assessment. Are there any threats encroaching
on your faith or the faith of those coming behind you? Jot down any
personal or cultural examples of the following:

A mockery or teasing about your faith choices or someone else's:

....

....

....

....

Opposition or oppression regarding your faith choices or someone
else's:

....

....

....

....

A powerful influence threatening to sway you or someone else from
the faith:

....

....

....

....

How is God asking you to courageously take a stand (rather than stay quiet) against threats?

....
....
....
....
....

Of the people you have influence over, who most needs to be reminded of the worth of God's inheritance? How will you wisely steward your influence?

....
....
....
....
....

God holds us responsible for how we steward our influence. Will you stand against the threats encroaching on your faith or that of others? Will you live like it's true that your inheritance, kept in heaven, is of infinite value?

Slaves or Sons?

Mornings were very stressful back when my kids were in elementary school, mostly because of how adamant I was about fitting Bible time into our morning routine. After beds were made, teeth brushed, hair combed, and breakfast inhaled, I sat them down on the living room sofas, opened my Bible, and taught them the truth to anchor their souls.

I'm sure there are things my kids retained, but what they remember most is squirming in their seats, afraid to interrupt me and say, "Uh, Mom . . . the bus will be here in one minute." Then what I remember is them bolting to the door, the moment I said, "Amen."

Looking back, I think I was convinced it was all up to me—there with my white-knuckled grip on my Bible—to mother my kids into the family of God. I was the one who had to make them listen. I had to win their hearts. *I* had to secure their place in the Book of Life.

But spiritual life is not something we can coerce in ourselves, nor in others. As in Sarah's story, our white knuckles of self-reliance only produce slaves, not sons.

Abraham's Two Sons

Read Genesis 16:1–2 (csb) and circle which of the following is correct:

> **Sarah said, "Perhaps through Hagar I can build more slaves."**
>
> **Sarah said, "Perhaps through Hagar I can build a family."**

Read Genesis 21:10 (csʙ) and circle which of the following is correct:

Sarah said to Abraham, "Drive out this slave with her son!"

Sarah said to Abraham, "Drive out this slave with my son!"

How did Sarah's plan and perspective change in the time between these two verses?

....

....

....

How did God's plan change in the time between these two verses?

....

....

....

Heirs of the Promise

Let's take a step back and consider the whole story once more, then we'll talk about how we can avoid Sarah's mistake.

First, who are God's heirs, and what has he promised them? They are the children of Abraham who will inherit the whole world (Romans 4:13). And how do we become these heirs? Like Abraham and Sarah, we believe God's promises with faith.

Back when the knowledge of God was being snuffed out across the face of the earth, God promised Abram and Sarai—a moon-worshiping, childless couple—that he would make of them a great nation, and they believed him! Their faith began not with doing some audacious thing, but with believing some audacious promises and living like they were true. The Abrams put feet to their faith and moved a thousand miles to the land God showed them, then lived in tents for the rest of their lives. Decades later, God gave them a miracle baby—the first of a long line of descendants, which led to the offspring Jesus.

Jesus was unlike any son born to a woman; he was sinless and didn't deserve sin's consequence of death. He died on the cross, not for his sin but for ours. God promises that Jesus's death counts as our penalty, his blood washes away our sin, and his eternal life and inheritance is ours to share. We become Abraham's children when we believe these audacious promises from God, and live like they're true.

Sister, if you believe God's promises about Jesus, then you, too, are an heir of all he promised to Abraham. You are one of God's people, restored to his presence, who will one day dwell with him in that shalom-filled place. And now, one of your God-given purposes is to be a spiritual mother—welcoming others as sons and daughters of Abraham, heirs of the promise. But mothers, beware. There's a certain tendency that we see first in Sarah, and then in many other instances throughout the Bible. It's this habit of producing slaves, not sons.

The Bullies of Galatia

Remember Paul's letter to the non-Jewish church in Galatia? This letter was written in response to a sharp argument going on about who could and couldn't be counted as sons of Abraham. Some Jewish people were bullying the Galatians, saying, "You think you can be one of us without doing all the stuff we Jews do?"

It was because, for hundreds of years, the Jews—or the blood relatives of Abraham and Sarah—had followed God's laws that were given back in the days of the Wildernites. There were hundreds of moral and ceremonial laws, which drastically set the Jewish people apart from other nations. But somewhere along the line, these Jews had begun to be shaped by these laws and rules, instead of God's promises.

Paul used the story of Sarah and Hagar to bring clarity to what was at stake.

Who does and doesn't receive the promised inheritance, according to Paul in Galatians 3:18?

....

....

....

....

Read Galatians 4:22–31.

Choose the correct word. Verse 22 says:

Ishmael was born to a slave | free woman.

Isaac was born to a slave | free woman.

Choose the correct word. Verses 23 and 29 say:

Ishmael was born of the flesh | promise.

Isaac was born of the flesh | promise.

Which of Abraham's sons represents us and why (v. 31)?

....

....

....

....

Briefly tell the story Paul is referring to in verse 29 (from Genesis 21:8–10).

....

....

....

....

....

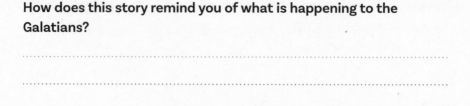

How does this story remind you of what is happening to the Galatians?

....

....

....

In response to the Jews who were bullying the Galatians into being shaped by God's laws, not his promises, Paul refers back to the story of Ishmael, saying, "Do you really want to be the *slave* in the story? Wouldn't you rather be the *son* of promise?"

I imagine it made the Jews as mad as hornets to be compared to the slaves, not sons. But Paul didn't care. He just wanted the Galatians to be free. He says, "For freedom, Christ set us free. Stand firm, then, and don't submit again to a yoke of slavery" (Galatians 5:1 CSB).

Hagar was a slave. Her son represented what Abraham and Sarah could do in self-reliance, without God. But Sarah was free. Her son represented what only God could do. When the slave son began bullying the son of promise, Sarah stood firm and demanded a split in the family tree. Then the slave son was sent away, and the son of promise remained.

Producing Slaves, Not Sons

As we consider growing the family of God, we—like the Galatians— must remember: only God can produce a true son, and only true sons get the eternal inheritance.

Sister, this is the truth, but I don't think we believe it.

As I look around, I see us producing lots of godly *looking* families and churches. We're the moms and grandmas who look over shoulders, monitor screens, search messages, and erupt over what we find. We're the wives and mothers-in-law and ministry leaders who use a condescending gasp or a roll of the eyes to leverage our "righteous" influence.

We're the church ladies and coworkers and social media posters who prompt and prod and punish the world with our Bible verses and viewpoints.

But then I look around again, and I see our kids squirming because the bus is coming and we're still reading verses. I see our new believers withdrawing from the Bible study and small groups, feeling like they'll never know their Bibles well enough or be able to scrub their lives pure enough. I see our young adults bolting for the door as soon as they can no longer be coerced into the pew. I observe all of this and wonder if we've forgotten: coercion doesn't produce sons, it produces slaves. This, too, is illustrated in Sarah's story.

In *Control Girl*, I wrote, "Quite frankly, a Control Girl mom can produce a pretty convincing imitation Christian, and this she can do *without* God. But a true child of God—the one who gets the inheritance—can't be produced by a controlling mom. His birth into God's family is like the birth of Isaac. It involves a miracle produced by God and no one else."

As spiritual mothers, we cannot coerce life. Only God can.

If you (like me) realize that your efforts to push and prod have given others the impression that freedom exists outside the church, please don't despair. If you've watched your own dear ones bolt for faith's door, please don't lose hope. Our God is able, and he delights in doing what our own efforts never could. God alone brings supernatural life. God wants us to believe his promises, live like they're true, and influence others to do the same.

Take inventory of your spiritual mothering.

Who have you had the privilege of influencing with the story of Jesus?

....

....

How have you tried to coerce others to follow God?

....

....

....

....

Who might think of you as a spiritual bully? What have you demanded they do or not do?

....

....

....

....

Who are you begging God to bring to spiritual life?

....

....

....

....

How would you behave differently if you believed others' salvation was God's work, not yours?

....

....

....

....

A New Son

In week 3, I told you about my seven-year-old responding to the gospel after that chock-full day of sin. Here's the part I didn't tell you.

After Bible time, when Cade indicated he wanted to be saved, Ken and I sent the other kids to bed and leaned in close to hear Cade's heart. But our independent little boy had other plans. He said, "I want you guys to go into the office and talk really loud, so you can't hear me ask the Lord Jesus to be my Savior."

We complied and went to the office, and a few minutes later, we were called back in by a grinning boy, who knew his heart was washed clean. A new son of the promise had been born, and though there's a sense in which I've gotten to be his spiritual mother, I had nothing to do with his spiritual birth. I wasn't even in the room!

How will you make room for God to bring new daughters and sons into the family of God today?

Considering Him Faithful

Sarah finally got to hold in her arms the laughter God had brought to life. God's faithfulness was tangible and sweet. But when Ishmael mocked little Isaac, Sarah saw Ishmael for what he had always been: a threat to Isaac's inheritance. Ishmael was sent away, and Isaac remained as the son of promise. Through him, God would keep (and has) his other promises.

RETELL

Summarize the story of Isaac's birth and the party conflict, using these quotes to guide you:

"God has made laughter for me..." (Genesis 21:6)

"Who would have said to Abraham that Sarah would nurse children?" (Genesis 21:7)

"Drive out this slave with her son...!" (Genesis 21:10 csb)

"Whatever Sarah says to you, listen to her..." (Genesis 21:12 csb)

....

....

....

....

....

....

....

....

....

....

....

....

REFLECT

Review some key points from the week and reflect on how God is inviting you to respond.

God is not dependent on our faith; he could have caused Sarah to wake up pregnant at age eighty-nine. Instead, he required her faith—the active kind. Sarah made herself vulnerable enough to hope for a baby.

How is your faith being stretched by a difficult or impossible situation? How does it require vulnerability to even hope?

....

....

....

....

How might God be waiting for you to respond with active faith before he unleashes his power? Or how do you see yourself growing because you *have* acted in faith?

....

....

....

....

Faith doesn't ignore doubts; it just gives more weight to God's faithfulness, asking, "Is anything too wonderful for God?" When we "consider," or stack up all of God's promises and his perfect track record, we shift from doubt to faith.

Which doubts are keeping you from faith? Here are some common ones:

If God loves me, why has he denied or taken the thing I want?

Where was God when _____ happened?

I can't see or hear God. How can I know he's real?

I don't see how God can bring anything good from _____.

....
....
....
....
....
....
....
....
....
....
....
....
....
....
....
....

Are you ready to experience that tipping point of faith? Consider any evidence in Sarah's story, in the rest of the Bible, in the lives of people you know, or even in creation that are contrary to your doubts. Remember that when we consider God's power and character, it creates a tipping point of faith. We give more weight to faith after considering all God has done.

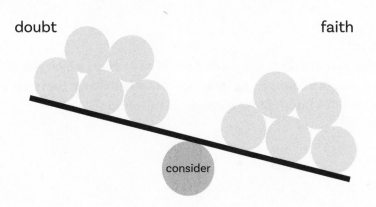

Sarah's laughter has gone from cynical to delighted. From skeptical to amazed. As she invites others to laugh with her, we see how God has transformed her insecurity, envy, and sorrow into lighthearted rejoicing over what only God could have done. For believers, this is just a taste of what is to come.

How are you afraid of being laughed at? How has your cynicism or skepticism kept you closed off to God or others?

How has God been transforming your insecurity, envy, or sorrow as you've studied Sarah's story?

....

....

....

....

....

What is something that only God could have done, which you're able to laugh about and delight over? How has God grown your confidence in his faithfulness through this situation?

....

....

....

....

....

....

When Ishmael mocks Isaac at the party, Sarah gets a glimpse at where this is all headed and demands that Ishmael leave.

Ishmael was her idea in the first place, but only because she lacked faith that God would fulfill his promise. Now it's her idea to send Ishmael away because she is filled with faith that God will fulfill his promise. Her reaction is proportionate to the value she puts on the inheritance.

Sarah had fiery faith when her son's inheritance was threatened. Whose eternal inheritance is being threatened?

....

....

....

....

How does God want you to respond in proportion to the value of this inheritance?

....

....

....

....

A true child of God has a birth story like Isaac's. It involves a miracle of God, not the heavy-handed work of a controlling woman.

How have you tried to mother someone into the family of God by relying on yourself, not God? Share any regrets you have in a prayer to the Lord.

....

....

....

....

....

....

What would change if you believed that every child born into God's family is his work, not yours? What changes is God asking you to make today?

....

....

....

....

....

....

....

REHEARSE

In this final part of Sarah's story, God faithfully kept all of his promises—even against all odds. God gave Sarah a son, who—through a long line of descendants—led to the promised son, through whom all of us have been blessed.

How did God reveal his faithfulness to Sarah by keeping his promises to her?

....

....

....

....

....

Will you be shaped by God's promises? Choose one more meaningful promise from appendix 2 (page 291), along with a verse to memorize. Write them both below.

....

....

....

....

....

....

....

....

....

....

Conclusion

Shaped by God's Promises

Read Genesis 22:1–19.

I doubt Abraham told Sarah what God had asked of him. How could she have found strength to let go of her precious Laughter, had she known?

Abraham must have woken up with dread all three mornings. Saying yes to God can be sickeningly painful. But this time, Abraham chose faith, not fear. He put feet to his faith, and once again, set out—going without knowing.

Abraham reasoned carefully about what God was asking. He knew that all of God's promises hinged on the boy not dying, but living. So if God was asking him to offer his son, then God would bring his son back to life (Hebrews 11:19). Faith begins not with doing some audacious thing, but believing some audacious promise from God, then living like the promise will come true.

This logic-driven faith is what fueled Abraham's feet as he climbed the mountain, stacked the wood, bound the boy, took the knife . . . then came the voice from heaven: "Abraham, Abraham!" God intervened. The test was over. God was pleased.

A lamb was provided and a father received his son back. A mother, too.

Centuries later, another son born to Abraham and Sarah's line—the promised offspring—climbed the same mountain, but this time the son was not spared. Jesus was crushed. He gave his life, keeping God's promise to crush the power of death. Three days later God raised Jesus from the dead and restored his eternal life—just as he promises to do for me and you.

God's promises are like a set of parentheses; they always come in pairs. God keeps the promises. God invites us to live by faith, believing the promises will come true. Sister, are you ready to put feet to your faith? Don't let fear hold you back. Instead, lift your eyes to something better and be shaped by God's promises—for every one must come true!

Appendix 1

God's Promises That Shape Us

Consider three questions as you approach the promises of God:

1. Is it for a specific person or people?

In the notes down at the bottom of the page in my study Bible, I read one day, "Many will become pregnant without having sexual relations with a man."

Huh? I thought. *When's that going to be?*

I leaned closer (that font is tiny!) and realized it was an "r" not an "n." *Mary* will become pregnant, not *many*.

Now that I'm over fifty, I've learned that glasses are not optional. Nor is it optional to apply Bible promises generally that were meant for someone specific. It's obvious we shouldn't claim God's promises about Mary or Sarah's pregnancies. But as we study Sarah's story, we'll also need to be careful about making the application that God always rescues his daughters from danger, or he always honors them in the end. I'm sure you can think of instances when someone *wasn't* rescued or *hasn't* been honored in this lifetime. This was true even of Jesus!

However, even God's fulfilled promises to other people (like those to Abraham and Sarah) help grow our faith in God's promises that are for us in particular.

2. Is it a principle or a promise?

God never changes (Malachi 3:6), which means that there is often a principle about his character for us to cling to, even if his promise was meant for somebody else.

Here's an example. God promised the Israelites that he would restore the years that the locusts had eaten (Joel 2:25). Now, it could be very hurtful to offer this as a promise to those suffering from crop damage after a locust outbreak. Joel 2:25 was a promise God made to Israel at a specific time. However, the principle is the same: Our God is a restoring God. When we cry out to him in repentance, he often does make up for years lost to rebellion, sin, or selfishness. See how the principle applies?

We also mustn't confuse the Bible's promises with principles for right living. Suppose someone claimed as a promise the proverb that says those who give generously will lack nothing (Proverbs 22:9), and took out a huge loan to give as a gift. This would be the opposite of wise living, and afterward she'd probably lack a lot of things.

Principles aren't promises. We must notice the difference.

3. Is it conditional?

Not everyone is forgiven of their sin. Not everyone will receive eternal life. Not everyone is welcome in God's presence. Some of the most sobering verses in the Bible tell about some who think God's promises apply to them, yet hear Jesus say, "I never knew you. Depart from me" (Matthew 7:23). The promises of the Bible only belong to those who are "in Christ," and even then, some promises are conditional on our obedience or faithfulness. Keep an eye out for "if, then" statements, or promises that could be restated with an "if, then,"[1] and include these conditions when you cling to God's promises or give them to others.

Here and Now, Then and There

Most of our promises for the "here and now" are intangible. They apply to our spiritual lives. Paul wrote, "Though our outer self is wasting away, our inner self is being renewed day by day" (2 Corinthians 4:16). Think of these promises like moisturizer and vitamins to rejuvenate our inner selves; they give us the healthy glow of faith.

Our "then and there" promises, however, *are* tangible! We'll walk on the streets of that Garden City, pluck fruit from the tree of life, and enjoy sweet fellowship at the marriage supper of the Lamb. We have so much to cling to, both now and then, but we must be careful not to confuse the two.

We actually don't have many tangible promises for the here and now. Jesus told his disciples to expect disruption, conflict, and loss because of his name (Matthew 10:34–39), and promised, "Whoever *loses* his life for my sake will find it" (Matthew 10:39; emphasis added). We'll have losses here; we'll have life *there*.

Hebrews 11 gives two lists of people who lived by faith. List one, by faith, experienced miraculous gain: they conquered kingdoms, shut the mouths of lions, and quenched fire (vv. 33–34). List two, by faith, experienced horrific loss: they were beaten, imprisoned, and sawed in two (vv. 36–37). All were shaped by God's promises, even though many "did not receive what was promised, since God had provided something better" (Hebrews 11:39–40 CSB).

Sister, as you consider God's promises, leave room for the "something better." There are many parentheses still open as we wander this earth, waiting for the one to come.

Appendix 2

Promises for You

Below is an unfinished list; I left room for you to discover more. Also, I want you to have the joy of reading God's actual promises from your own Bible (these are summarized).

For my printable, "Praying the Promises," go to shannonpopkin.com/promises.

HERE AND NOW
Promises of Forgiveness and Salvation

Jesus is faithful to forgive my confessed sin. (1 John 1:9)

God forgives and blots out the record of my sin. (Isaiah 43:25; Romans 4:7)

God does not hold my forgiven sin against me. (Psalm 103:12; Hebrews 8:12)

I will not be condemned for my sin. I've crossed from death to life. (John 5:24; Romans 8:1)

I will escape the judgment of raging fire. (Hebrews 10:27; Revelation 20:15)

God, by his grace, forgives my sins and redeems my life. (Ephesians 1:6–8)

I cannot "out-sin" the riches of God's grace. (Ephesians 1:7)

God sees me as righteous. (2 Corinthians 5:21)

....

....

....

....

....

....

....

....

HERE AND NOW
Promises for Spiritual Life and Refreshment

The Spirit helps me, strengthens me, and is with me. (John 14:16; Ephesians 3:16–17)

I can find rest in Jesus. (Matthew 11:28)

God hears my prayers. (Matthew 7:7–11)

The resurrecting power of Jesus lives in me. (Romans 8:11)

The Spirit reminds me that I am God's child. (Romans 8:14–16)

God will never forsake me, so I have nothing to fear. (Isaiah 41:10; Hebrews 13:5)

God comforts me in all my troubles. (Psalm 23:4; 2 Corinthians 1:4)

Jesus gives me peace to guard my heart and mind. (John 14:27; Philippians 4:6–7)

Nothing can separate me from God's love. (Romans 8:39)

I am set free from sin's power. (Acts 13:39; Romans 6:6–7)

I have everything I need for godly living. (2 Peter 1:3)

My temporary troubles prepare me for eternal glory. (2 Corinthians 4:17)

I have spiritual armor to withstand the enemy's attacks. (Ephesians 6:10–17)

Jesus broke the devil's power, so I am no longer a slave to fear of death. (Hebrews 2:14–15)

The Holy Spirit in me guarantees my inheritance. (Ephesians 1:13–14)

....

....

....

....

....

....

....

....

THERE AND THEN
Promises of Heaven for Those in Christ

Like Jesus, I will be raised from the dead. (2 Corinthians 4:14)

God will bring me into glory. (Colossians 3:4)

There will no longer be any curse. (Revelation 22:3)

I will live with God forever in his Garden City, and I will see his face. (Revelation 21:1, 3; 22:4)

I will never die, grieve, cry, or experience pain ever again. (Revelation 21:4)

I will eat from the tree of life and drink from the water of life, and live forever. (John 3:16; Revelation 22:2, 14)

I will reign with Christ. (Revelation 5:10)

Anything I've lost because of Jesus will be restored a hundredfold. (Matthew 19:29)

My faithful living and generosity will be rewarded. (Matthew 6:4–18; 10:42; 16:27; Ephesians 6:8)

....

....

....

....

....

....

....

....

....

Acknowledgments

I'm so honored to work with the wonderful people at Our Daily Bread Publishing. Thanks in particular to Dawn Anderson, Sarah De Mey, JR Hudberg, and Kate Motaung. I'm blessed to partner with you in kingdom work.

I am incredibly grateful to my dear friends who prayed weekly as I wrote this study: Whitney, Lori, Sarah, Amy, Jamie, Angela, Kimberly, Carrie, Jane, Melissa, Cheryl, Reyna, Evelyn, Tereasa, Gail, Renell, and Brenda. Thanks also to Rachel, Cheyenne, Brian, Nancy, Libby, Aaron, Andrea, and others who helped me think carefully about God's promises and Sarah's beautiful story. Thanks to Sana Latrease, Heather Cofer, Gaby Puentes, and Jill Savage, who shared their powerful stories of faith.

Thanks especially to my sweet husband, Ken, who was the first to complete this study—one lesson at a time, as I wrote it. Thanks for encouraging and supporting me as I write. I am blessed to have you as my partner in ministry and in life.

And to my Lord, Jesus, who took my place on the cross, made a way for me to be blessed and not cursed, and promises me an eternal inheritance—how can I ever express enough gratitude? I can't wait to be with you in that Garden City, with its unshakable foundations.

Notes

WEEK 1: The People of the Promise

1. Kenneth A. Matthews, *The New American Commentary, Volume 1B* (Nashville: Broadman & Holman, 2005), 113.

2. Kent Hughes, *Genesis: Beginning and Blessing* (Wheaton, IL: Crossway, 2004), 178.

3. Mary Fairchild, "Christian Wedding Symbols: The Meaning Behind the Traditions," LearnReligions.com (updated June 3, 2020), https://www.learnreligions.com/christian-wedding-traditions-701948.

4. Marvin R. Wilson, *Our Father Abraham: Jewish Roots of the Christian Faith*, 2nd edition, (Grand Rapids , MI: William B. Eerdmans, 2021), 187.

5. John Piper, "The Unashamed God," Desiring God (July 1, 1997), https://www.desiringgod.org/articles/the-unashamed-god.

6. Nancy Guthrie, *Better Than Eden* (Wheaton, IL: Crossway, 2018), 14.

7. Kent Hughes writes, "Bethel, like Shechem, was home to an important Canaanite sanctuary to the god El, head of their pantheon. But, as in Shechem, Abram ignored this and built an altar to Yahweh 'and called up on the name of the LORD.' Abram publicly proclaimed the name of the Lord. . . . He proclaimed his faith. [Martin] Luther translated this 'preached' to convey the idea here. Abram's entourage was quite large. . . . So this was a very public event. The locals knew what was happening. Proclaiming

Yahweh's name would include extolling his great attributes and mighty works. Preach it, Abram!" Kent Hughes, *Genesis: Beginning and Blessing* (Wheaton, IL: Crossway, 2004), 187.

8. Guthrie, 126.

9. Allen P. Ross, "Genesis," in *The Bible Knowledge Commentary: An Exposition of the Scriptures*, ed. J. F. Walvoord and R. B. Zuck (Wheaton, IL: Victor Books, 1985), 47.

10. Charles Swindoll, *Abraham: One Nomad's Amazing Journey of Faith* (Carol Stream, IL: Tyndale, 2014), 17.

11. Michael Kruger, *Hebrews for You* (Epsom, England: The Good Book Company, 2021), 173.

12. Thanks also to Trina Cofer, who filled in some of the details of her amazing story via email.

WEEK 2: Betrayal and Rescue

1. "Walking the Bible," PBS, https://www.pbs.org/walkingthebible /timeline.html.

2. Kent Hughes, *Genesis: Beginning and Blessing* (Wheaton, IL: Crossway, 2004), 192.

3. Derek Kidner, *Genesis* (Downers Grove, IL: InterVarsity Press, 1967), 128.

WEEK 3: Shame and Control

1. Tim Mackie, "Humans Are . . . Trees?" *Bible Project Podcast*, July 26, 2021, 69:00, https://bibleproject.com/podcast/humans-are -trees-2/.

2. Abbey Wedgeworth, "Developing a Theology of Suffering with Abigail Dodds," October 7, 2020, https://www.abbeywedgeworth .com/held-podcast-show-notes/ep-010-developing-a-theology-of -suffering-with-abigail-dodds.

3. E. Randolph Richards and Richard James, *Misreading Scripture with Individualist Eyes* (Downers Grove, IL: Intervarsity Press, 2020), 4.

4. It's interesting to note that four of the twelve sons born to Jacob (the Abrams' grandson, father of the twelve tribes of Israel) are born this same way—through his wives' maids, Bilhah and Zilpah. See Genesis 30:3–12. But as we encounter polygamy, surrogacy, and slavery in the Bible it's important to remember that these passages are descriptive, not prescriptive.

5. In *How to Read the Bible as Literature*, Leland Ryken says we handicap our interpretation of biblical stories when we fail to consider its overarching framework and patterns. He writes, "In the absence of such framework, the story remains a series of disjointed and isolated fragments." Ryken quotes E. M. Forster, who suggests we begin at the end of a story and march backward to notice the cause and effect relationships between the story's events. For our purposes, its helpful to begin then in Genesis 21:12 with God supporting Sarah's demand to send teenage Ishmael away because he mocked Isaac. Starting there, where Ishmael is seen as a threat to Isaac's promised inheritance, we move backward through the story and see that the cause for this threat was Sarah's self-reliance in Genesis 16. Leland Ryken, *How to Read the Bible as Literature . . . and Get More Out of It* (Grand Rapids, MI: Zondervan, 1984), 44, 47, 49.

6. Tremper Longman III, *Genesis: The Story of God Commentary* (Grand Rapids, MI: Zondervan, 2016), 210.

7. Timothy Keller, *Galatians for You* (Epsom, England: The Good Book Company, 2013), 76.

8. Daniel Baldwin, "What to Do If You Find a Black Widow Spider," July 19, 2022, https://hawxpestcontrol.com/what-to-do-if-you -find-a-black-widow-spider/.

9. John H. Sailhamer, *The Pentateuch as Narrative: A Biblical-Theological Commentary* (Grand Rapids, MI: Zondervan, 1992), 154.

10. Derek Kidner, *Genesis* (Downers Grove, IL: InterVarsity Press, 1967), 137.

11. "The Head and the Neck," *My Big Fat Greek Wedding*, YouTube .com, https://www.youtube.com/watch?v=CJbC5AfxqPc.

12. Shannon Popkin, "How to Overcome My Desire to Control My Husband (Kelly Needham)," November 2, 2022, https://www .shannonpopkin.com/desire-to-control-my-husband/.

13. Timothy J. Keller, "Hagar and the Son," The Timothy Keller Sermon Archive (New York City: Redeemer Presbyterian Church, 2013), accessed through Logos Bible Software.

14. Robert Alter, *Genesis* (New York: W.W. Norton, 1996), 68.

15. Kent Hughes, *Genesis: Beginning and Blessing* (Wheaton, IL: Crossway, 2004), 240.

16. Hughes, 240.

WEEK 4: Renewed Hope

1. "The Letter Hey," Hebrew for Christians, https://www.hebrew 4christians.com/Grammar/Unit_One/Aleph-Bet/Hey/hey.html.

2. Robert Jamieson, "The First Book of Moses, Called Genesis," Blue Letter Bible, https://www.blueletterbible.org/Comm/jfb /Gen/Gen_018.cfm?a=18002.

3. Robert Alter, *Genesis* (New York: W.W. Norton, 1996), 79.

4. Derek Kidner, *Genesis* (Downers Grove, IL: InterVarsity Press, 1967), 141.

5. Timothy Keller, *Romans for You* (Epsom, England: The Good Book Company, 2014), 105.

6. Kent Hughes, *Genesis: Beginning and Blessing* (Wheaton, IL: Crossway, 2004), 257.

WEEK 5: Reverting to Fear

1. Timothy Keller, *Romans for You* (Epsom, England: The Good Book Company, 2014), 104–105.
2. Kristen Wetherell, *Fight Your Fears* (Bloomington, MN: Bethany House, 2020), 23.
3. Wetherell, 16, 18.
4. Kent Hughes, *Genesis: Beginning and Blessing* (Wheaton, IL: Crossway, 2004), 289.
5. Kenneth A. Matthews, *The New American Commentary, Volume 1B* (Nashville: Broadman & Holman, 2005), 258.

WEEK 6: Laughter and Perspective

1. Shannon Popkin, *Control Girl: Lessons on Surrendering Your Burden of Control from Seven Women in the Bible* (Grand Rapids, MI: Kregel Publications, 2017), 70.
2. Robert Alter, *Genesis* (New York: W.W. Norton, 1996), 98.

Appendix 1: God's Promises That Shape Us

1. Charles Swindoll, *Abraham: One Nomad's Amazing Journey of Faith* (Carol Stream, IL: Tyndale, 2014), 175.

Spread the Word
by Doing One Thing.

- Give a copy of this book as a gift.
- Share the QR code link via your social media.
- Write a review of this book on your blog, favorite bookseller's website, or at ODB.org/store.
- Recommend this book to your church, small group, or book club.

Connect with us. ⓕ ⓞ

Our Daily Bread Publishing
PO Box 3566, Grand Rapids, MI 49501, USA
Email: books@odb.org

Love God. Love Others.

with  Our Daily Bread®

Your gift changes lives.

Connect with us. ⓕ ⓘ

Our Daily Bread Publishing
PO Box 3566, Grand Rapids, MI 49501, USA
Email: books@odb.org